THE INVISIBLE THREAT

THE
INVISIBLE
THREAT

A PROFESSIONAL FIDUCIARY'S GUIDE
TO UNSEEN CHALLENGES IN WEALTH MANAGEMENT

MATTHEW EBY WITH JOANNE EBY

THE INVISIBLE THREAT
A Professional Fiduciary's Guide to Unseen Challenges in Wealth Management

FIRST EDITION

ISBN   978-1-5445-4691-9   *Hardcover*
       978-1-5445-4690-2   *Paperback*
       978-1-5445-4692-6   *Ebook*

For Ben

CONTENTS

WHAT IS THE INVISIBLE THREAT AND WHERE DOES IT COME FROM?

N SEPTEMBER 2008, THE BANKRUPTCY OF LEHMAN Brothers sent shockwaves through Wall Street, triggering a crisis that almost brought down the global financial system.

Much has been written about the causes of Lehman's collapse and specifically the bursting of the housing bubble, but there's more to this story. The crisis, which came to be known as the Great Recession (and is considered the worst financial crisis since the Great Depression), has been seen by some as potentially linked to the passage of the Gramm–Leach–Bliley Act of 1999 (GLBA). The GLBA, commonly referred to as the Financial Services Modernization Act, was touted by politicians at the time as a law that would bring convenient one-stop shopping to financial consumers for banking, securities, and insurance—like what Costco and Wal-Mart are to retail shoppers.[1] It is the law that essentially enabled financial institutions to diversify business operations beyond their own industry's traditional boundaries.

In particular, this legislation repealed Sections 20 and 32 of the Glass–Steagall Act of 1933 (GSA). The GSA was the Depression-era regulation aimed to protect vulnerable Americans and their savings. Sections 20 and 32 put up a kind of barrier between commercial and investment bank activities to, in effect, separate Wall Street from Main Street.[2] However, GSA's intended separation eroded over the decades. As an example, Merrill, a broker-dealer firm, owned several insured depository institutions, a federal savings bank, and numerous state-chartered trust companies well before 1999.

The GLBA not only repealed Sections 20 and 32 of the GSA to allow for universal banking under one structure, it also added Section 4k to the Bank Holding Company Act to permit insured depository institutions (i.e., "banks") to affiliate with securities firms, insurance companies, and other entities engaged in activities that are "financial in nature." This was a key element that allowed financial firms to wear multiple hats at once and act as investment bank, commercial bank, insurance company, trust company, or any combination thereof.

While Lehman Brothers' downfall did not itself trigger, nor was it caused by, the GLBA (Lehman was not a bank holding company and Wall Street had used commercial paper and other capital markets funding tools to originate and buy mortgage loans well before its passage in 1999), nonetheless the news of the bankruptcy brought the post-GLBA financial services industry to the forefront, with many questioning whether the repeal of Sections 20 and 32 of the GSA caused the crisis.

As the wider economic crisis unfolded between 2008 and 2009, the government intervened with bailouts, forced mergers, and other measures to support financially-stressed institutions. But these efforts failed to account for the underlying issues associated with the post-1999 reality that, after the floodgates had been opened, many financial institutions rushed into unfamiliar areas of banking or securities business without seeming to know very much about them!

Here's how it went down in those years from 1999 to 2008 and beyond.

The new millennium witnessed a period of mega-mergers in the financial services industry, with the six largest banks growing their assets between 1997 to 2008.[3] However, most of the "too-big-to-fail" institutions the government intervened with were actually pure investment banks or insurance companies, not universal banks. So it's hard to pin the Great Recession on the GLBA in any kind of causal way. What became clear in the aftermath, however, according to the Financial Crisis Inquiry Commission, was that those large investment banks "focused their activities increasingly on risky trading activities that produced hefty profits [...] Like Icarus, they never feared flying ever closer to the sun."[4]

What's not in dispute is the fact that the past two decades have seen banking, insurance, and investment firms move to diversify, including into the trust industry, long a rather staid business that only traditional banks engaged in. The resulting organizational combinations—colloquially referred to as "wealth management" services and often created under either a bank or financial holding company[5]—began to take on new and increasing levels of fiduciary risk.

However, because these new wealth management organizations were essentially novices to trust products and services, they were caught unawares. Much of the fiduciary risk remained hidden to them. So, naturally, they struggled in their attempts to administer the trust business, eventually finding themselves in the crosshairs of bank examiners.

Just like in chemistry, all the mixing of elements and ingredients had introduced certain new business combinations that were poorly suited for one another. On the surface, it all seemed so exciting. But it was also extremely combustible. A ticking time bomb.

We saw that bomb go off in a big way in 2008. But the same ill-suited business combinations, along with unseen levels of fiduciary confusion, still plague financial institutions to this day. And the same issues that emerged in the post-GLBA era are still widely overlooked or misunderstood within the industry. In fact, many of today's wealth management organizations, whether they realize it or not, exist in a permanent state of instability, where an impending crisis could always be just around the corner.

This is what we mean when we talk of the Invisible Threat.

The threat doesn't come from the risk itself—in fact, it's essential that trust institutions take fiduciary risks—but rather the not-knowing.

The threat is also compounded by the tendency within these firms to misidentify the culprit. When a gap emerges, as it inevitably does, between expectations and outcomes, it's often assumed that this must be due to some technical issue. More often than not, however, the real problems stem from these organizations not *adapting* their complex and diverse business environment to fiduciary requirements.

Therefore, it follows that the real solutions lie not in fixing technical issues, but in mobilizing the adaptive work.[6] What's the difference?

TECHNICAL VS. ADAPTIVE WORK

Let's say you're a professional fiduciary facing a regulatory compliance challenge. You seek out an expert who provides a step-by-step plan to meet the requirements. This situation is clearly technical: the problem is well-defined, and the solution straightforward. Once the expert provides the solution, all the fiduciary has to do is follow the instructions and get back to business. Very little effort or adjustment is needed on the fiduciary's part.

That's technical work in a nutshell: addressing a clear problem with a straightforward solution.

Adaptive work, however, is much trickier. It deals with complex problems that lack easy answers. Take, for example, a brokerage firm that wants to offer comprehensive wealth management services, including trustee services, and chooses to accomplish this by acquiring a trust company. In this case, the brokerage firm can't just rely on an expert to provide a ready-made solution. Instead, the newly formed wealth management organization, now consisting of both brokerage and trust businesses, must take on the responsibility of making adaptive changes: establishing a unified wealth management culture, overhauling the business model, and more. While an expert can guide the process, there's no clear-cut roadmap to success. Instead, the newly combined organization and the expert must work together to identify the adaptive challenges ahead and create appropriate solutions. Unlike technical fixes, adaptive work requires significant effort and adjustment; it demands a shift in values, beliefs, and behaviors.

Unfortunately, this is not what usually happens. All too often, the conversion to wealth management services is mistakenly viewed as strictly a technical challenge, simply a matter of adding the newly acquired trust company to the corporate structure and branding it a wealth management firm. At best, there may be corporate talk of a "merger of equals," but in reality, what typically occurs is the acquiring firm dictates terms to the acquired firm. In our example of a brokerage firm acquiring a trust company, the newly combined wealth management organization just ends up operating in silos of brokerage and trust, with each side resenting the other because the organization avoided the adaptive work. This hampers their ability to navigate and adjust to evolving circumstances, representing a missed opportunity for growth and change, and leaving them vulnerable to the Invisible Threat.

We know because we see this every day.

WHO WE ARE

As consultants to the trust and wealth management community, we—Matt and Joanne—have seen firsthand the many challenges faced by professionals in the field and have helped clients, including some of the biggest names in the business, navigate the complexities of the fiduciary industry.

Organizations that work in this space come to us for help when they're grappling with their vision: their expectations (that never seem to match their reality) and their blind spots, as well as the general ineffectiveness of known solutions. We also advise them on such matters as conflicting client expectations, deviations from fiduciary duty, operational disruptions, and regulatory challenges.

Through it all—over the course of our years doing this kind of work—we've come to believe that the traditional methods for achieving growth and enduring success are largely ineffective for solving the problems that trust organizations face in today's wealth management industry.

We believe what's needed is a multi-disciplinary, adaptive approach.

Now, with our first book, we draw upon decades of industry

experience (including years of boots-on-the-ground, hands-on involvement in the industry), as well as our roles as educators (teaching classes for Cannon Financial Institute, delivering custom client training programs, and speaking at industry events in the US and internationally), to shine an important light on the Invisible Threat facing financial institutions in today's wealth management industry—and to call upon readers to embrace the need for adaptive change in today's complex world.

In the chapters ahead, we will cover all of this and more, sharing insights and proven strategies for organizations confronting the toughest, most persistent problems, as well as exploring the important distinction between technical solutions for routine challenges and adaptive solutions for non-routine challenges.

Other topics include the importance of formal and informal authority when developing strategies and assessing available resources, as well as the crucial shift in mindset needed for adaptive challenges. Without this requisite change in thinking, it's very hard to change behavior, and organizations will likely continue to use the same hammer, so to speak—the same blunt tools they always have—to try to fix what invariably looks to them like just the same old nails in need of pounding.

But it doesn't have to be this way. In fact, when we look at today's most successful trust companies, we see that they are the ones able to truly visualize their fiduciary landscape and make adaptive changes to take advantage of the new business opportunities.

What we *won't* be doing in this volume, however, is diving deeply into the technical realm of trusts, trust companies, and trust regulations. In contrast to that kind of nuts-and-bolts how-to guide, what we're putting forth here is aimed at something broader, something that provokes genuine traction: helping *make the invisible visible*, so you and your organization can move toward finally solving those intractable, seemingly insurmountable problems.

Ultimately, our hope is that you take away from this book a new way of looking at the entire landscape for providing professional trust services within today's wealth management industry.

We want you to feel empowered to make good decisions and optimize your practices toward ridding your organization of the Invisible Threat in this complex and fast-changing environment.

Understanding the hidden assumptions causing the gap between what you want and what you have is the first step toward closing that gap.

CHAPTER 1

SEEING HIDDEN ASSUMPTIONS

MAGINE TRYING TO NAVIGATE THROUGH DENSE FOG, where each step forward is filled with uncertainty. You can't see what's ahead, and every move feels risky. This is the reality for many trust organizations operating in today's financial world: they're stumbling blindly through complex terrain, hindered by many unseen obstacles. They can't see through the fog of outdated assumptions, which obscures the true challenges they face. In fact, these assumptions hide an Invisible Threat, leading to missteps and unexpected problems.

In this chapter, we will begin to lift that fog. By revealing blind spots and making the invisible visible, you will start to gain the insight needed to see yourself and your organization more clearly. You will uncover hidden assumptions you didn't know you had—the ones causing the gap between what your organization wants and what it actually has—and you will learn how to adapt in ways you never thought possible.

Every organization has a set of deeply ingrained values, beliefs, and behaviors, often inherited from years of industry norms and practices. These beliefs shape how individuals working in the organization see and tackle problems, creating a familiar, shared view of reality. But within this comfort zone of well-known values, beliefs, and behaviors lie blind spots—hidden assumptions that block true understanding and effective action. These are not just minor oversights; they are the core reasons why the expectations of your organization don't match reality, and why those within the organization—*like you*—feel stuck in an endless cycle of frustration, trying to fix a never-ending series of problems. To break free, you need to identify and challenge these assumptions, embracing a mindset that seeks out what's hidden and addresses the real complexities of today's fiduciary landscape. Seeing these hidden assumptions is the crucial first step toward bridging the gap between where your organization is and where it wants to be.

CHALLENGE ASSUMPTIONS, CHANGE OUTCOMES.

Before we dig into how to uncover these hidden assumptions, let's take a moment to clarify what we mean by assumptions versus beliefs. For the purposes of this book, we consider an assumption as an acceptance, *without proof*, that something is true or not, and a belief as not just an acceptance but a *conviction*, also without proof, that something is true or not.

Think about it: how many times have you and your team come up with what seemed like the perfect approach, directly addressing a problem, only to find yourselves back at square one when the fix didn't pan out? It's not because you lack the skills or determination. It's because the real issues are often buried beneath layers of outdated thinking and hidden behind blind spots.

Consider, for example, the *assumption*, i.e., acceptance without proof, that your legacy trust accounting system is up to the task of meeting the current demands of your trust clients. This assumption is ingrained within your organization: after all, the system has always been satisfactory in the past and your staff are comfortable with its capabilities. Seems reasonable enough, right? What's the problem? Initially, this assumption might indeed be helpful because it saves time and resources by eliminating the necessity to convert to a more modern trust accounting platform. But when your legacy system can't keep up with today's high-tech, high-touch, high-speed client expectations, the assumption becomes harmful, leading to unhappy clients and loss of business. By constantly challenging your assumptions and exploring solutions, you can better align your *values*, like excellent customer service, with your *behaviors*, like making sure your system meets your customers' evolving needs.

In the example above, by challenging assumptions your organization discovered their trust accounting system was *not* meeting client expectations. This awareness allows organizations to recognize when an assumption is no longer helpful. Once that fact is known, it becomes easy to solve the problem because the solution is also known: convert to a modern trust accounting system. While the process of implementing that known solution is going to be hard—system conversions typically are—the technical solution is a well-known one and industry experts skilled in system conversions can assist.

Uncovering hidden assumptions and beliefs will help you see the full picture. You will start to understand why certain problems keep recurring and why some solutions have become obsolete. This clarity will also empower you to approach challenges adaptively (rather than continuing to apply technical solutions to every problem), using methodologies in tune with the ever-evolving demands of the "new" trust company in today's wealth management industry.

In the chapters ahead, we'll guide you through this counterintuitive process, helping you make the invisible visible by challenging hidden assumptions in order to turn your persistent problems into opportunities for growth and success.

THE JOURNEY: HOW DID WE GET HERE AND WHAT'S THE WAY FORWARD?

If you're like most of our clients, you're coming to this book, we assume, because you have a problem within your trust organization. It is also likely that your trust company is affiliated with, or handles trust business for, a wealth management organization that includes either a broker-dealer firm overseen by the Financial Industry Regulatory Authority (FINRA)[7] or an investment adviser firm registered with the Securities and Exchange Commission (SEC), or both.[8] A well-known example of a wealth management organization is Bank of America, which expanded its banking business nationwide with a series of acquisitions at the start of the new millennium. In particular, when the bank acquired US Trust in 2007, it extended its reach into the private-banking-for-high-net-worth-individuals business, of which trust services are naturally a huge part. Then, in 2009, Bank of America acquired the brokerage firm Merrill Lynch. A peek at their website today shows that they offer broker-dealer, investment advisor, and trust services—all under their wealth management banner—among other business lines, including, of course, consumer banking.

As described in the Introduction, this is the kind of convergence of complex lines of business expanded in the financial services industry post-GLBA. While securities firms were already operating within such complex business structures even before the GLBA, after its passage the absence of Sections 20 and 32 of the GSA was seen by some to have created a "reckless, risk-taking, profit-focused culture on Wall Street." Joseph Stiglitz, an economic Nobel Prize laureate, included this risk-taking, profit-focused cultural shift as one of five major contributing factors to the Great Recession.[9] He noted that the most important consequence was indirect but impacted an entire work culture. That's because the changes in the laws brought a different mindset, a more reckless ethos, to today's wealth management industry, with its focus on risk-taking, short-term profits, and de-prioritization of client interests.[10]

Bank of America and other behemoths like Citigroup—bailed out by the government as "too big to fail" during the 2008/2009 financial crisis—were far from the only financial institutions to expand their service offerings, whether before or after passage of the GLBA. Depending on their size and the nature of their business, many other banks acquired, merged with, or were themselves acquired by securities firms, including registered investment advisers (RIA) or broker-dealers. Bank or financial holdings companies are often a way to "hold," under a parent organization, these business combinations that cross regulatory lines, including banking, trust, securities, asset management, and insurance businesses.[11]

In the post-GLBA era, banks looked to increase profits by expanding their traditional client base and started offering not only their well-established banking services but a whole platter of what came to be known as "wealth management" services.[12] They realized that to remain competitive they needed to increase their product offerings to include non-bank services; if they didn't, they might risk losing the customer base they had worked so hard to build. The writing was on the wall, as more and more customers sought the ease of that one-stop-shopping concept for all their financial needs. Similarly, broker-dealer or RIA firms that didn't have an affiliated bank able to provide their customers with trust services learned they stood to lose business if their wealthy clients transferred their assets to trust accounts.

Put this all together and you see how the post-GLBA era became an environment where financial services organizations, including banks, RIAs, and broker-dealers, became incentivized to combine businesses that didn't, and still don't, fit well together.

As one of our colleagues shared with us, "What happened in the eighties and nineties, and may have been exacerbated by passage of the GLBA, is that broker-dealer securities salespeople and stock jockeys got control of trust companies...and were clueless. Over time there have been lots of other factors as well—like online trading, elimination of commissions, and other threats to the traditional broker-dealer business model that pushed them to fee-based advisory services and trust companies."[13]

Add the reckless culture of today's wealth management industry to the once staid and very conservative trust industry, and it's easy to see how these ill-suited business combinations pose a very real Invisible Threat.

But the desire for more lucrative business means executives will overlook the continuing, and potentially fatal, cultural and philosophical differences between those ill-suited business combinations.[14] Moreover, it has become the norm for bank trust departments, or non-bank state or OCC-chartered trust companies, to be directly affiliated with, or provide services to, firms on the securities side of the industry, including SEC registered investment adviser firms or broker-dealer firms overseen by FINRA. Customers, it seems, do have an appreciation for one-stop shopping.

So yes, you are not imagining it: your trust organization is struggling to thrive.

Perhaps you are reading this book because, like so many other bank trust departments or non-bank state or OCC-chartered trust companies (which we will take the liberty throughout this book of collectively referring to as "professional fiduciary firms") in today's wealth management industry, you are experiencing a problem, or many problems, because the folks in your organization on the FINRA and SEC sides of the business *just don't get* the trust business.

While you already have a trust license that permits you to provide professional fiduciary services, you are struggling to make a real go of it. Maybe you're dealing with audit or examination issues. Or pressure from upper management to increase revenue and profits. Meanwhile, you're also having trouble hiring and retaining qualified staff to handle the trust administration side of the business. It's possible your personnel are hampered by legacy trust accounting systems unable to keep up with the high-tech, high-touch, high-speed expectations of your securities industry partnerships—those registered investment adviser or broker-dealer firms who often own the client relationships and refer your professional fiduciary services to them. Those self-same clients have now gotten used to lightning-fast financial services, without realizing, for example, that your professional fiduciary firm is obliged to take the time to ensure distribution of funds from trust and estate accounts is indeed permitted. Not only that, but you also have to locate and secure trust and estate assets, then obtain appropriate signed paperwork and other documentation from the client, before any funds can be released.

It's a lot. But all of these challenges can be boiled down to a single thing: the gap between what you want and what you have. In the broadest sense, the problem your professional fiduciary organization is facing can be described as: the difference between the expectations for your organization and the realities it's currently struggling with.

Yes, every situation is unique, but this difference, or gap, is the common denominator. It's what prevents you from seeing a way forward to success. On our end, it's the problem that animates virtually all the client work we do. And for your part, when faced with this problem of the expectations placed on your trust organization versus the current reality you struggle with on a daily basis, the big question, of course, is what do you do to close that gap? Where do you even start?

The three standard business options to problem-solving are: (1) just continue along doing what you're doing and resign yourself to the gap; (2) convince the Board of Directors that this is what happens in every organization these days and lower everyone's expectations to make the gap seem narrower; or (3) try to change the current reality by solving the specific problems your organization faces. Think of this as the standard decision-tree your organization might use to narrow down potential solutions.

We say these are the standard options to problem-solving because they are the ones we see professional fiduciary firms pick time and time again. It wouldn't surprise us at all if you've already attempted all three approaches—to the very same problem. Chances are you've tried them many times over. That's the point: even though you and your team have likely come up with all sorts of ideas and solutions to fix problems as they crop up, you're stuck in the same daily cycle of struggling with those problems. None of the standard options have provided lasting solutions.

Maybe you're like some of our clients who tell us they can only ever react to issues, when what they really want instead is to be able to see things in advance and fix them once and for all, *before* they turn into major problems. One client told us it's like they're playing a daily game of Whack-a-Mole, trying to spot problems as soon as they pop up so they can knock them back down, only to continually have new ones (or even the same ones!) burst up.

We've had many clients tell us they were tired of being "reactive." They wanted to be proactive. And it's for this same reason that you and your firm may have already gravitated instinctively to the third of the standard business options: trying to change the current reality, and solving specific problems as they pop up. It makes sense that you would. After all, this approach probably worked well for you at some point in the past. But it is also likely that it only worked before when the problem needing to be fixed was one that called for a technical solution. Can that be said about the problems you're currently seeing?

You may think so, but what we have discovered over our decades in this industry is that often our clients can't see a problem for what it really is. What's more: they do not realize that they can not see it. That's why they keep trying to solve what they *assume* to be the problem, and this goes on for months and even years, leaving them incredibly frustrated.

What they can't see is that there is another approach beyond the three standard business options. We call this "3′ Prime," because unlike the regular third option where you try to solve the problems your organization faces, with 3′ Prime you're trying to change your current reality by fixing the person having the problem: namely, you.

How do you tackle a problem you can't even see? You need a high-voltage solution, and by choosing the 3′ Prime path, you're embracing the bold, frankly counterintuitive notion that it is *you* who must adapt in order to see the problem. This is something very new for many clients we work with, and we have come to learn that it can be quite controversial indeed.

But it really is the only way forward in such a scenario. You can't solve your problem without understanding what it is and what's causing it. And you certainly can't do that if you can't even see it. Adding the 3′ Prime Option to the decision tree is how you get there. But in order to succeed with this approach, you have to examine the hidden assumptions and beliefs that you and your organization may be holding.

WHY HIDDEN ASSUMPTIONS ARE SO DAMAGING

MATT: Back when I was an eighth grader at Catholic school in my hometown of Burbank, Illinois, I had this one teacher, a nun like all our teachers, who I'll always remember even though this was MANY decades ago. Her name was Sister Mary Jerome, and she was new to the school that year. So, unlike the other teachers, she didn't know me from before, didn't know my family, didn't know my sisters, Lynn and Di, who had gone to the same school. And we got off to a rather bad start, Sister Mary Jerome and I. She was my history teacher, but history was a brand-new subject for me, and I wasn't great at keeping up with all the reading assignments.

Here's the thing, though: from almost the very beginning of our time together, she just *assumed* I was a ne'er-do-well. Actually, her favorite description to use on us students who didn't keep up with our homework was "booby doob"—and it was usually me on the receiving end of those words!

It may sound silly now, but this all really got to me. I felt like she was making me out to be something I wasn't. Yes, I often failed to complete my homework. But I was good at other subjects like math and science. Reading just wasn't my thing;

I had a hard time with it. Did she really have to be so mean? It wasn't like I was disruptive in class. But that didn't stop her from criticizing me, calling me a booby doob, and telling me I'd never amount to anything.

I dreaded going to her class and tried my best to avoid her in the hallways and playground. Even though she was probably only five feet tall, she scared me! I remember she wore square blocky glasses that made it seem she could see right through me. It was like she had my number, had already formed her opinion of me—had just assumed I was a lazy, no-good booby doob—and her *assumption* wasn't going to change.

That's the thing about assumptions: the person making them usually doesn't even realize they have the assumption. They just accept, without proof, that something happens to be the way it is. Which is the reason we refer to these as "hidden" assumptions— the person can't *see* that it is an assumption, they just accept it. To Sister Mary Jerome, me being a booby doob was just a fact. Meanwhile, my fear of her, combined with my ongoing struggle with the homework assignments, created its own kind of combustible situation. I became very nervous that I would fail the class, which only made things worse.

Sister Mary Jerome continued to treat me miserably through the first half of the school year. But then something big happened: my mom died.

My mother had been diagnosed with cancer three years earlier, when I was ten. In those months leading up to her passing, her health had taken a turn for the worse. She was in the hospital a lot, which meant she was less involved with the family, with me and my younger brother who went to the same school. Meanwhile, my dad was understandably stressed out. He spent a lot of time at the hospital with my mom those last few months, which took him away from his job—and from us kids. There was less money in the house, and with all the medical expenses, our family's financial situation had become pretty bleak.

During this difficult period, we basically watched my mom die. She got thinner and thinner as the cancer advanced. It was lung cancer, inoperable at the time, so there was nothing we could do but watch her fade away. By the time Christmas came around that year, our home had become her hospice.

She died on January 2, 1969, the first day back at school after the Christmas break. She was only forty-six and it was a big deal to have someone so young from our parish community die like that. They announced it at school, and the funeral home was right across from the convent where the nuns lived. So the teachers came over to pay their respects and it was then that I saw Sister Mary Jerome. Her tear-filled eyes locked on mine, and she came right over and wrapped her arms around me. It was such a different experience than I'd had with her before. She just kept hugging me and repeating the words "I didn't know, I didn't know."

Even more remarkable: after that, it was like she had become my caretaker, my guardian. All of a sudden, it was me she picked to do teacher-pet things for her like handing out papers to the class or erasing the blackboard at the end of day. The transformation was night and day. Not only did she no longer scare me, but I even began to confide in her and share my struggles with reading. She ended up coaching me in reading a few afternoons a week. During this time, my classmates commented that our reading assignments had become shorter. It was something I had noticed too; I think she reduced the load because she was looking out for me. And I was also genuinely improving at reading. Within a couple of months, I had become one of the best students in her class.

What lay behind all these changes in how Sister Mary Jerome

treated me? It's clear to me now that when my mom died, Sister Mary Jerome realized she had been harboring hidden assumptions about me. Initially, she had seen a *problem*—a gap between her expectations for me as one of her pupils and the reality of my performance in her class—and had chalked it up to me being a bad student unwilling to complete the class assignments. But after learning of my mom's death, she realized that there had likely been lots of other factors she couldn't see. Because she couldn't see them, she had assumed, mistakenly as it turned out, that I was a booby doob. What she eventually came to understand, however, was that I'd been struggling with something very real and difficult, and that the Eby household had been dealing with a great deal of pain and challenge. It wasn't just that I was some ne'er-do-well booby doob who didn't care.

Sister Mary Jerome adapted. She challenged, and invalidated, her assumption about me and was then able to see me through a new lens. Rather than seeing me through her "lazy booby doob" lens, she now saw me through a different lens, her "vulnerable child" lens, and it brought out the caretaker in her. She recognized I was a student who needed to be seen differently. Recognized that what my thirteen-year-old self really needed was her help and guidance, not her disdain. Once she saw me through a different lens, she changed her whole mindset about me. For the rest of the school year, she took care of me by treating me like a good student, then helping me become one. I went from dreading her class to looking forward to it.

But if Sister Mary Jerome had never challenged her hidden assumption in this way, if she had never changed her lens when she looked at me, this happy outcome—of solving the problem and closing the gap (between her expectations for me and the reality)—would have remained out of reach.

She could have stuck with the status quo and done nothing

about the gap. Or she could have lowered her expectations of me and written me off as a lost cause. Either way, I would have continued to live in fear of my teacher and felt worse with each passing day about my incomplete assignments, while she would have just let me glide through to the end of the year. I am eternally grateful she didn't.

HIDDEN ASSUMPTIONS IN FIDUCIARY ORGANIZATIONS

Key to understanding and addressing the Invisible Threat lurking beneath trust and wealth management organizations is seeing what's really going on under the surface. Where are the blind spots?

Just like Sister Mary Jerome missed this at first, so do many professional fiduciary firms inside a more complex wealth management environment. Not surprisingly, many of these are newly chartered de novo trust companies created specifically to provide trust services for affiliated securities-regulated firms under a larger wealth management corporate structure. Odds are these professional fiduciary firms are being established primarily to use the trust license as a wrapper to be able to provide investment management or brokerage services for trust assets. When these broader organizations then fail to achieve the synergies and successes expected from the addition of a trust company, it leads to internal frustration and finger pointing. What people don't realize, however, is that the gap between their expectations for the organization as a whole (including the securities regulated lines of business *and* the professional fiduciary firm) and their current reality is likely caused by hidden assumptions they're not even aware of. They only see what's on the surface, and they only see what they're expecting to see, which leads the organization to spend lots of time and money chasing the wrong solutions.

What are some of these hidden assumptions they're missing?

For one, the people inside these complex wealth management organizations may assume their role is the same as it used to be, and still think of themselves in a narrow way as traditional investment advisers, financial advisors, registered representatives, trust officers, or whatever role they had in the past.

To be clear, this does not always lead to disaster. Say, for example, a registered investment adviser firm partners with a brokerage firm to take advantage of the synergies created when the former uses the latter for custody and training. The people on both sides, in both firms, are certainly already aware of the basics of the regulatory environment, because they're both under the umbrella of the SEC. Yes, there are some complexities, especially on the brokerage side, which is regulated by the more prescriptive FINRA rules. But generally, this particular combination of investment management and brokerage business tends to produce the good results everyone expects.

What happens, though, when the same successful wealth management organization then acquires an existing professional fiduciary firm, or establishes a de novo trust company, for the sole purpose of using trust powers as a wrapper for investment management or brokerage services, especially for existing trusts they know their customers already have?

Here's where things get tricky. The people in the securities-regulated division of the organization may continue to think of themselves in the traditional way, in whatever role they had with their client previously, whether as an investment adviser or broker. Even when that same client becomes the grantor of a trust, for which the affiliated professional fiduciary firm provides trust services, the person on the securities side still wants to provide the same advisory or brokerage service they always have, in the same way. They continue to view the client as the owner of the account. And they continue to believe their job is to bring the client, the grantor of the trust, the same level of fiduciary service the client always received in the past—what we refer to as the *small-f* fiduciary approach that securities regulated advisers take. They know their affiliated trust company has a fiduciary responsibility, and likely assume it is a shared responsibility. They may also labor under the hidden assumption that the financial advisor remains responsible for the relationship, continuing to have the *conviction* that the "client" is the person who can fire them.

What they often cannot see, however, what remains hidden, is the real difference between the small-f fiduciary responsibilities for securities regulated firms and what we call the *big-F* Fiduciary Lens that a professional fiduciary firm is bound by its fiduciary *duty* to see through and embody.

People in the trust industry understand that the grantor—the individual who established and funded the trust—is not necessarily the "client." They could be sole or co-trustee of the trust, and the trust's current beneficiary. However, the trust may also have other beneficiaries, a purpose beyond the life of that individual who established and funded the trust. Looking through the big-F Fiduciary Lens, people inside the professional fiduciary firm harbor no assumptions about who the client is. They clearly see, for all intents and purposes, that the "client" is the *trust itself.*

Bound up in the hidden assumption across this same wealth management group that people's roles are the same as they used to be, there likely exists another assumption, also ubiquitous through the organization, that risk in general is inherently bad and can only be negative—a liability for the organization. Something to be reduced or avoided at all costs. Yet for professional fiduciary firms, as we mentioned in the Introduction, this is an assumption that can, and should be, challenged.

After all, professional fiduciary firms, by default, accept fiduciary risk from the very moment they're appointed as trustee. It is just a fact of the trust business. So it's essential that professional fiduciary firms understand this and don't shy away from but instead actively embrace this fiduciary risk. People who work in the trust industry understand that fiduciary risk is inherent to their business. They know the Invisible Threat *doesn't* come from the fiduciary risk associated with the accounts they accept.

While all professional fiduciary firms know in theory that they too have accepted fiduciary risk—it's a fact of the business—where the Invisible Threat comes in is with a different kind of knowing (or rather *not*-knowing), a danger lurking in the fog. Even traditional trust departments of traditional banks, those with decades or even a century of experience in providing trust services, worry there may be fiduciary exposure that they can't see and have unknowingly accepted. For trust companies inside a wealth management organization, the Invisible Threat is far worse. In these more complex environments, it is likely the folks working inside the securities regulated business cannot see what the trust company people see: a vast pool of fiduciary risk they do not have full control over, bubbling and percolating under their very noses. Why can the trust company people see what the others can't? Because they're looking at the situation through their big-F Fiduciary Lens and trying their best to manage (not eliminate) their fiduciary exposure. They're exactly right in their approach. Unfortunately, they are often stymied by the hidden assumptions of the broader organization where it's assumed the grantor is the client (and if things get messy, it's assumed they can just "quit" serving the client).

Perhaps what we see with our clients most of all is this: in trying to diagnose problems within their professional fiduciary firm, people can only see the symptoms of their problems—the issues that rise to the surface—and so they focus their attention on alleviating those pain points. They pour resources into trying to eliminate surface issues through repeated technical solutions, only to find that the gap they are trying to close remains as wide as ever.

Why do their efforts fail? Just like Sister Mary Jerome, they miss the fact that what they're seeing is just a symptom of an underlying condition. They labor under the hidden assumption that the symptom *is* the problem.

We've seen this dynamic play out with many clients over the years, some in spectacular fashion. This was especially true prior to the expiration of estate and gift tax laws in 2012 when there was such a demand for trust services that existing trust companies couldn't keep up with the tsunami of trusts being established before the year-end deadline, new trust companies were being formed, and broker-dealer firms were shopping to quickly acquire trust companies.

What follows is a story based on an amalgam of client issues we have actually seen, many that date back to that time period, with a fictional person we'll call George. The details of his story, which we will now share with you, are particularly relevant and instructive—and we suspect many of you will relate in a big way.

"HOW COULD THIS BE?"

George remembered the chaotic excitement of those first few days after it was announced that the brokerage firm he worked for had just acquired a trust company. While many of his colleagues on the brokerage team seemed clueless about the implications of the deal, George believed that overall the news was good. His views on the matter aligned with those of corporate, who were incredibly enthusiastic and painted the acquisition as a way to retain and even expand their brokerage firm's client base and ultimately increase profits. *Not to mention my bonus*, George thought to himself.

"This is a golden opportunity for us," the CEO explained in a company-wide meeting a week later. All of their existing clients' financial accounts, their brokerage accounts, other investment accounts, including their revocable trusts (and potentially future trusts), could now be under one roof, and the newly acquired trust business would surely lead to growth for the brokerage arm of the company, where George worked. He assumed that trusts always hold a lot of wealth, wealth that would need to be custodied and invested in the marketplace, leading to more brokerage commissions all round.

Six months later, the deal finally closed. Another company-wide meeting was called to announce the news and explain how the trust company would change its name to align with the brokerage firm's overall brand but keep its own separate legal structure. George didn't pay much attention to the mumbo jumbo; he believed he was above the details. He had "people" to take care of that. The real excitement for him was the prospect of selling trust services alongside other offerings to his brokerage clients.

His mind reeled, imagining the opportunities for his team to earn commissions on those sizeable trust accounts. It was all George could think about after the meeting as he walked back to his office, where he was surprised to find four people standing outside his door—his boss, his boss's boss, and two of the company's lawyers. As he approached the group, George's boss asked him to join them in the conference room down the hall.

There, George was finally offered that long-sought promotion to the ranks of the executive team. They asked him to lead the newly acquired trust business as president.

His boss's boss explained that George's primary task was to ensure a successful transition of the new company into the culture of the brokerage firm, and that they expected the addition of the trust business to bring twenty-five percent growth to the company's bottom line after the first year. After the second year, it should be more than double that.

Then, George's own boss spoke and assured him and everyone in the room that George was just the right guy to take this on. He was the man who could get the job done.

Tell me something I don't know, George thought, haughtily. In his mind, the promotion was long overdue. He saw it as his ticket to a board seat after years of interminable waiting.

George noticed that neither lawyer said anything during the meeting. But when he was walking back to his office afterwards, one turned to him and, speaking softly, mentioned that if George ever wanted to know anything about the legal aspects of the new trust business, he could stop by any time to discuss.

In the moment, George thought nothing of the comment. He was preoccupied with his own achievement and all he wanted to do was bask in the news of his promotion. George felt optimistic about the enduring success of his firm, a decades-old, mid-size brokerage firm, unflashy but well respected across the financial securities industry. He had always viewed it, institutionally, as a place he could thrive, even before it acquired the trust company. And with the acquisition, and George's promotion to president, his future seemed bright.

Some two years later, George sat in his office remembering the lawyer's words. He hadn't ever taken the lawyer up on his offer to discuss the trust business. But perhaps it was time to do so. George certainly needed the help. Over the past two years, everything had turned out so differently than expected with the trust company. Somehow the mood had grown darker across the entire organization. For George personally, it seemed like Corporate was on his back all the time. At first, they were on him about the bottom line, which was indeed going in the wrong general direction. Not only had George failed to achieve the first year's goal of adding twenty-five percent, he was staring at a second year of financials with the trust business operating at a loss and relying on the brokerage side of the business to keep it afloat.

After the first year of losses, George had gone to his bosses with what he believed was needed to fix the problem, explaining to them why they had no choice but to raise the trust company's fees. They took his advice. But one year later, after twelve months of having charged those higher rates, the trust company's overall profitability was trending down at an even faster pace than before. George's solution had turned out to be a flop. How could this be? Not only had the fee increases failed to solve the profitability problem, but the situation had gotten worse!

George was facing other challenges as well. Why were so many clients leaving? Some of the best trust accounts were lost because disgruntled grantors and beneficiaries removed them as trustee and appointed other trust companies to administer their trusts. George thought the fee increases were the problem and tried to negotiate lower fees for those accounts, but apparently fees were the least of the reasons for the general dissatisfaction with their trustee services.

Around the same time, George had discovered to his horror that advisors in the brokerage division, the very same people he used to pal around with at work, were in fact recommending to clients who inquired about the trust company services that they'd be better off acting as their own trustee or engaging an outside trustee, while the brokerage division could continue to handle all of their custody and advisory needs. Ouch.

George had also wondered why he continued to be hit with numerous major audit and exam findings. Before taking on this new role, he had never, not once, had to worry about such matters. When he was on the brokerage side, he was aware FINRA came in from time to time to kick the tires and make sure everything was on the up-and-up. He kept up with the firm's compliance requirements, attending trainings and reporting all his personal trading. But never as a manager on that side of the business had George been handed a damning report with items alarmingly labeled "Matters Requiring Board Attention." Those words definitely grabbed his attention the first time he saw them. He was pretty terrified when he had to present that first negative report to the Board of Directors. But oddly, they didn't seem to care. All they asked about was when he was going to get the issues with the bottom line resolved.

What a mess. George wondered how this could be happening, and to him of all people? How was he going to fix all these things and not lose his job?

First, he knew he had to stir up new business to make up for the lost trust accounts. So, assuming he knew best, George hired a salesperson to promote the trust company's services, since it seemed the brokers were incapable of doing so themselves. It was the logical next move, George realized, telling himself, "I've never been wrong before."

Next, he had to deal with the rats' nest of weird issues from the most recent audit report, like how they incorrectly set up the custody accounts for the trusts on the brokerage platform using the client's name.

George had tried to learn about such details from the staff

that came over with the acquisition. But to George it seemed like they were just lost and angry. While he had originally planned for a seamless transfer of the acquired trust accounts to the brokerage platform, the trust company staff had insisted on keeping their own system, which cost a lot to maintain. George thought it was crazy. Why use two systems, the trust system and the brokerage platform, for what seemed like identical information? Not only did both systems have stocks, bonds, and other securities held in the accounts, they were the very same securities—and the same accounts! Maintaining the same securities on the trust system as well as the brokerage platform was expensive in itself because there was a separate fee just to get those securities priced. Never mind the cost and hassle of having to duplicate on the trust system each and every transaction that took place on the brokerage platform.

And don't even get me started on the dual cash thing, George thought as he stared at the audit report. The trust company staff kept telling him they needed to keep their own system because of dual cash. George still didn't get it. *Cash is cash. Who cares about dividing it into separate streams of income or principal?*

George had also given up on trying to convince the trust company staff that the brokerage platform could do everything they needed and provide them with all the relevant income numbers. George assumed he was right: the brokerage system tracked dividends, bond interest, and capital gains just as well as any custody platform. But somehow for the trust company staff, this was just not good enough. George could see that he had lost the battle. So, he moved on and took a different tack, going hat in hand to his bosses to plead for more time to get the bottom line moving in the right direction.

But looking at the most recent audit report, it seemed there was still a problem with the brokerage custody platform. Something about using the wrong name when the brokerage division set up the trust accounts on their platform.

Just that morning, George had talked about this with the most senior trust officer on his staff, and she tried to explain to him, not for the first time, that a trust is not a legal entity. It is simply an agreement between the grantor and the trustee, and as such, cannot legally own anything. Which is why, she said, when setting up the accounts on the brokerage platform, they needed to list the name of the trust company as trustee of the trust. She told him, yet again, that when the trust company accepted appointment as trustee of the trust, under the trust agreement they essentially had to take "ownership" of the trust assets on behalf of the trust. For the accounts on the brokerage platform, having the name of the trust company on the official paperwork was how they evidenced ownership.

As for the problem of client statements, another issue raised in the audit report, at least this was something George understood. Or so he thought. Apparently, according to the senior trust officer, statements had to go to practically everyone and their cousin who had any association with a trust. Okay, George didn't realize all that. But at least the statements themselves were something George knew a thing or two about from his years on the brokerage side of the business. He grasped the basics, knew that client statements had to go out on a regular basis. Of course they did: there were rules about that, and it seemed they were the same rules on the trust company side. His confusion was around how *many* of the darn things had to be sent out and why the statements sent from the brokerage platform were apparently not the right ones.

So he asked the senior trust officer about this, and she explained that sending a statement from the brokerage platform directly to the grantor, *and only to that grantor*, did not satisfy the requirements for the trust company to send statements to all qualified beneficiaries. When George then asked what made a beneficiary qualified, he got the answer that had now started to make him cringe every time he heard it. "Well," she explained, "it depends."

If George had a dollar for every time he'd heard those words since taking over the trust company, he could throw the whole wad at the bottom line and maybe his bosses would finally get off his back. The morning of that conversation with his senior trust officer, he decided not to follow up by asking *what* it depended on, because he knew he'd get the answer he dreaded most: "applicable law!" He did ask her, though, why the auditors were fussing so much about not sending statements to all of those qualified beneficiaries. "Look," George told her, "I know for a fact that with the seven accounts mentioned in this report, the client specifically asked that we send the statements from the trust system to him and his wife only, not his children." She just shrugged and told him that the client's preference was irrelevant: the children were all grown adults and the applicable law in this case required that the adult children receive their own copies.

At that, George just rolled his eyes and walked away, as he was known to do. The senior trust officer looked relieved and beat a hasty retreat. As he walked back to his office, George grimaced uncomfortably. The senior trust officer was one of the few remaining staff from the original group that had come over with the acquired trust company. She was a hard worker and even though he wasn't crazy about her attitude, George could not afford to lose her—for now. He could tell she was unhappy and might hand in her notice any day. This was the last thing he needed, especially given his struggles with hiring new staff.

During his time running the trust business, he'd discovered that staffing a trust company was not at all the same thing as hiring for the brokerage industry. It turned out that most young people fresh out of college preferred the excitement of the latter. *And who wouldn't?* George thought. *There was much more opportunity to earn the big bucks on that side of the business.* Even when he was able to bring on someone straight out of college, it seemed to take forever to get them up to speed on what needed to be done. Mistakes abounded, even in the most entry-level trust operations positions. And luring a seasoned trust officer away from another trust company had proved very challenging. It seemed that throwing a lot of money their way did not guarantee they would take the job offer. Even if they did, it was hard to keep those people happy. They always complained that the brokerage side of the firm wanted them to do things differently than they were used to. They also complained to George directly that they were being asked to do things that applicable trust laws did not allow them to do. George couldn't understand why they always seemed so flustered and whiny.

He still wasn't quite sure he understood all the latest audit issues but having just heard the words "legal" and "legally" and the dreaded "applicable law" thing from the senior trust officer, again his brain pulled out of its memory banks what the company lawyer had said to him the day he got the big job. Clearly, it was past time for George to take him up on his offer and stop by his office to get some advice on the legal aspects of the trust business. But with all the challenges the trust company was facing, he also hated to have to admit to anyone inside the organization how he was struggling.

He knew these were serious problems, and the longer they continued wreaking havoc on his business, the more frustrated George became. He was at the end of his rope but vowed not to fall into despair. Instead, he assured himself he could tackle the problems one by one with smart, common-sense solutions.

For example, there was nothing fun about getting hit by major audit and exam findings, but George took comfort in the fact that if he could just fix the issues in the audit report, the other problems the examiners wanted the Board to pay attention to would go away, leaving one less headache for him to have to deal with.

And it was the same all around. Yes, the accumulation of problems was challenging, but individually they were conquerable. *I can do this,* he told himself. *If there is anyone who can turn the tide, it's me! No matter how bad things may seem at the moment.*

DON'T SWEAT THE SYMPTOMS

How do you think this story turned out for George?

We can all appreciate his determination but also see how his energies are misplaced. That's because we know he is focusing on the wrong things, trying to alleviate pain points and take pressure off, while missing what's most important, the underlying issues.

In our experience, everyone is vulnerable to this impulse. Even if just to buy some time. When faced with problems like George's, we're compelled to immediately stamp out the thing in front of us we don't like. We focus on removing the thing we can see, in the hope that this will also eliminate the pain point facing our business. This behavior, instinctive and well-intentioned as it may be, has the unfortunate consequence of preventing us from looking deeper to identify what's truly causing the gap between expectations and reality.

This is the great irony of George's situation. His bosses hold him to a set of fairly daunting but standard expectations: that he'll run the trust company successfully, improve the bottom line for the entire firm, keep the trust clients satisfied, and avoid audit issues and exam findings. So it's not such a surprise or even a knock against him that George finds himself struggling from the start. But he doesn't know what to do with that struggle, how to deal with it. He can't figure out why his reality is so far off from his expectations for the trust business, and in his zeal to fix all the problems, George harbors dangerous assumptions hidden within him.

Being able to see hidden assumptions and understand why we make them, specifically in the context of the professional fiduciary firm in today's wealth management industry, is what this book is all about.

For example, when we see George make the invalid assumption that the problem of losing trust accounts to other trust companies can be fixed by hiring a salesperson to sell more trust business, it's not that he's totally wrong—no one wants to see their best accounts leave. And yes, adding a salesperson to bring in new business will staunch the bleeding of lost revenue. However, George's lack of understanding means he accepts, without proof, that adding new trust accounts will offset the lost revenue and not hurt the bottom line. He does not see this for what it really is, an assumption, and so he cannot challenge it—and therefore misses the essential opportunity to understand he is not looking at his trust business through the right lens.

More specifically, given his prior experience with the brokerage firm, George assumes he can view the trust company through the same lens he is already so familiar with. In fact, the brokerage lens is likely the *only* lens George has available to him. He's not aware of what he lacks, or that a different lens even exists. After all, he was told from the beginning that his job was to ensure a successful transition of the trust company into the culture of the brokerage firm. George's assumption that new accounts will offset the lost business might be helpful if he were on the brokerage side, but is actually harmful on the trust side. Acceptance of new trust business is complex, time consuming, and may come with higher levels of fiduciary risk. Not understanding *why* the lost business left in the first place also means new accounts could head out the door as quickly as they come in.

WE HAVE TO SEE OUR HIDDEN ASSUMPTIONS BEFORE WE CAN CHALLENGE THEM.

By exerting such a strong pull on us, our hidden assumptions and beliefs can be hard to see.

As consultants, we've encountered this most often with the problem of staffing inside trust companies, one of the same problems George experienced. Many professional fiduciary firms assume they have a staffing problem. Typically, they don't have enough staff, or they can't retain the right staff. George was no different. He tried to get more resources and believed scarcity was to blame for his company's struggles in this arena.

But what he, and all of us, need to understand is that it's usually not about scarcity or lack of resources. In fact, from our own experience with this particular issue over the years, we've come to believe that for most people working in the trust industry, they show up day after day with the best of intentions, trying to do the very best job they can. No one *wants* to be a lousy employee, and people who work in the trust business are genuinely passionate about the industry and their own role in it. Skilled trust professionals understand they are guardians of the trusts, and they take that responsibility seriously.

So why all the problems with staffing? We've seen this issue come to the fore particularly in those wealth management organizations made up of an ill-suited combination of businesses. On the trust side of the organization are skilled trust professionals struggling to do the right thing in this wealth management context. But where pressures start to emerge—not only from grantors or beneficiaries, which is typical for trust companies, but also from those working on the RIA or broker-dealer side—is when they push for things based on their own hidden assumptions around the trust business.

Both sides want to do what's best for the client and the issue is rarely bad staff. They're typically really good staff, on both sides; they're just trapped by their own hidden assumptions.

What about you? When it comes to this exciting journey you are now embarking on with this book—where you are finally learning how to solve these problems and navigate the complexities of this fascinating industry—we are calling on you, here at the beginning, to take the time to not just ponder the hidden assumptions you may be holding but actively challenge them, to see if they are helpful or harmful.

You have to always be wary of your first instincts. Always look for your blind spots. Try to see your current reality for what it actually is. This is key to seeing *why* there remains such a gap between your expectations and the current realities. That act of seeing is just the first step to ultimately narrowing the gap and achieving what is expected. That's your end goal. But before you get there, you'll have to first grapple with your own lens and how you see the problems you're facing. Whether it be staffing, audits, or other problems, the road to fixing these challenges hinge on your ability to lift the fog.

When adaptive change is needed, you can not close the gap or solve the problem without first being able to see your own hidden assumptions and beliefs.

Last, but not least, it's really, really hard to do this on your own, especially when the required lens may be unavailable. You'll need the right help to continue on this journey.

SEEING HIDDEN ASSUMPTIONS

1. THE PROBLEM LIES IN HIDDEN ASSUMPTIONS

Standard Approach and Outcome:
- Focus on solving visible symptoms of problems.
- Example: George raises trust company fees to improve profitability, but situation worsens because underlying issues weren't addressed.
- Outcome: Problems appear to be addressed temporarily but reoccur.

Counterintuitive Approach and Expected Outcome:
- Identify and address hidden assumptions underlying the problems.
- Example: Understand that hidden assumptions about roles and responsibilities creates gaps between expectations and reality, as seen with George's struggle to integrate trust company's practices into brokerage firm.
- Expected Outcome: Lasting solutions that resolve the root causes of issues.

2. FIX THE PERSON HAVING THE PROBLEM

Standard Approach and Outcome:
- Fix problem directly with technical solution.
- Example: George hires salesperson to boost new business but fails to see deeper integration issues between the trust and brokerage divisions.
- Outcome: Temporary fixes that do not address the core problem.

Counterintuitive Approach and Expected Outcome:

- Change the person experiencing the problem by adapting their perspective.
- Example: George realizes that adapting his own management approach is crucial to addressing underlying issues within the trust company.
- Expected Outcome: A deeper understanding of the problem leading to more effective solutions.

3. CHANGE THE LENS AND THE IDENTITY

Standard Approach and Outcome:

- Maintain static professional roles and perspectives.
- Example: Brokerage staff continue to see themselves solely as brokers, not adapting to the new trust services they must now understand and offer.
- Outcome: Limited ability to navigate new challenges.

Counterintuitive Approach and Expected Outcome:

- Adopt a new lens and change one's identity within the organization.
- Example: Recognize how the fiduciary lens differs from the small-f fiduciary approach and how this affects trust company operations and expectations.
- Expected Outcome: Enhanced ability to adapt and thrive in a dynamic environment.

CHAPTER 2

GETTING THE RIGHT HELP

A S WE SAW WITH GEORGE, THERE IS A STRONG TENDENCY within organizations to try to close the gap (between what they want and what they have) by fixing what's on the surface, the symptoms—or pain points—rather than look beneath the surface to see and challenge their underlying assumptions. To challenge his own hidden assumptions would have required George to use a different lens to view the trust company. It would have required a shift in his whole way of thinking. What held George back was his reluctance to admit his uncertainty or potentially be blamed for having pursued the wrong solutions to the company's problems. But chasing the pain-points rather than *seeing* the hidden assumptions only leads to a Whack-a-Mole approach that rarely yields the intended results. Remember how George and his firm raised fees, hired a new salesperson, and even started questioning the quality and loyalty of existing personnel. In a way, this typical approach makes logical sense. It's intuitive. But that's also what makes it dangerous. It's what happens when assumptions are seen—accepted without proof—as facts.

It's also what happens when professional fiduciary firms, or individual professional fiduciaries, try to fix the symptoms or pain points *directly*, using the same technical solutions over and over again on the same issues, yet somehow expecting, and hoping, to get different outcomes.

In this chapter, we will show why it's so important for professional fiduciary firms, or even those acting in an individual capacity as a trustee, not just to procure help, but the *right* help.

Before we get to that, however, it's worth taking a step back to look at why it's so hard sometimes—not just for professional fiduciary firms and not just in the workplace but with all human endeavors—to see what is needed in a given situation when we are in the thick of things. We have all had this experience in our lives at one time or another where someone comes along and opens our eyes to an action we need to take or path we need to go down—even without knowing we needed any help. You'll see this in Matt's story where he couldn't even see he had a problem until someone else opened his eyes.

THE HELP I NEEDED

MATT: I had just gotten out of the military and was feeling a little lost. Although I did have a job, as a materials handler at a metal manufacturing plant, it was only part-time and wasn't very interesting or challenging. This was back in Burbank, Illinois, but by this point we—me, my brother, Mike, and our older sister, Diane—were living in a different house, next door to Diane's mother-in-law, who had basically taken us Eby siblings under her care after our own mom died. She had virtually adopted us, welcoming all of us into not just her family but into her heart. We called her "Mom Florez" or even just "Mom" for short.

Diane ended up dating, and ultimately marrying her high school sweetheart, Derek, who just so happened to be Mom Florez's son, making our familial connection that much stronger.

My job at the metal manufacturing plant was near home, but again, it was a pretty casual gig and I didn't take it very seriously. I didn't have much going on at this time and was mostly just working there and otherwise hanging out. Like many returning vets, I didn't quite know what to do with myself in the absence of the structure and discipline of the armed forces.

Somehow, Mom Florez easily saw all of this, likely because her two oldest sons, my "adopted" brothers Rory and Robin, were military veterans too. One afternoon when it was just her and me at the Florez house—as it often was at that time of day since her own younger kids, Daria and Scott, were still at school—she gave me an ultimatum. By that point, a couple months after I had returned from military service, she had grown sick of seeing me bum around day after day.

We were sitting at the kitchen table, enjoying a cup of tea together as I remember it, when out of the blue she pulled out a stack of papers and slid them across the kitchen table towards me. It was an application to the local community college. She had already filled it all out. All I had to do, she explained, was sign and submit it. But then came the kicker: if I didn't, if I refused, I would no longer be welcome in her home. Just like she had been willing to do for other members of our extended family before me, Mom Florez was not only threatening, but was actually willing, to kick me out—for my own good.

Whoa! Talk about a reality check. But in retrospect, not only was she absolutely justified in her actions (as if she needed my approval!) but it made total sense that she of all people would have taken such a hard line. Mom Florez was someone who took education very seriously. She had never gotten a chance when she was younger to pursue a degree, so later in life had taken the opportunity to attend the same community college where she was now insisting I go. Through her own experience at the college, she had also gotten to know some of the school administrators, and that was how this new application wound up first in her hands and then in mine.

Mom Florez had little patience for laziness of any kind. As the matriarch of this grand blended family, she had no choice but to run a tight ship—which is exactly what she did. In fact, she was a bit like a drill sergeant herself. She could be very stern, that's for sure. But we loved her. And she was giving me the tough love I didn't realize I'd needed.

As usual, she didn't mince words. She told me I was wasting my life and if I didn't do this, didn't go to college, I'd never amount to anything. These were the same words, you might recall, that Sister Mary Jerome had used on me years earlier. This time it was Mom Florez, part of my own family, saying these things. She told me it was my choice and if I wanted to throw my life away, I could go right ahead. But not in her house. If I went against her wishes, there would be no more sipping tea together across the kitchen table. She refused to be a silent accomplice to my bad choices.

That was all I needed to hear. It was her way of motivating me—and it worked. I enrolled in and attended classes at the community college, then continued down the educational (and then career) path that Mom Florez had helped set in motion.

There's a moral to this story that goes beyond just the importance of education or work ethic. What Mom Florez did was recognize what I really needed when I couldn't see it myself. She knew I could no longer put off the next stage of my life. But I had no idea—until she slid the college application to me and helped me see what I needed to do.

It took her giving me that kick for me to see I first had to change my mindset. She was "the right help" at the right time. And with Mom Florez' intervention, ultimately I was able to adapt by shifting my lens to that of a student, which led to a lifetime of learning. This changed my environment, my expectations for myself, and helped me solve a number of problems I was dealing with during that period of my life.

THE HELP YOU NEED

Who will be your Mom Florez?

If you're like many of the people we work with at professional fiduciary firms, at a certain point you realize the Whack-a-Mole approach to problem-solving isn't working. Your company may have been hiring people, firing people, implementing, then backing out of, process changes, getting new technologies—in other words, going through the same cycles we see over and over again. But eventually people at your firm will stop and think: *Okay, there has to be something else, something concrete we're lacking. We must not have the right stuff. There must be some questions we're not asking, some answers we're missing.* This is when you reach out for help.

Let's pause for a moment here to pick up on the business decision-tree from Chapter 1: you may recall that the very first choice you had to make was whether you even needed to try to understand and address the gap between expectations and reality *at all.* But you may also remember from the opening chapter that there is another choice altogether, one that all too often gets overlooked. We're talking here about the "third rail" approach, what we referred to as the 3′ Prime Option, which focuses on the person having the problem: namely, *you.*

You know you want to make a positive change in your organization, to finally fix the problems and close that gap between what you want and what you have. Toward this end, you may have also decided to pursue an external solution. But what you need to remember at this important juncture is that, as we alluded to in the first chapter, there are two distinct approaches for the kind of positive change you seek: technical or adaptive solutions. Let's explore these both a little further.

Technical solutions are well-known, routine solutions to the kind of common problems that professional fiduciary firms regularly face. That doesn't mean they're unimportant. Technical solutions are a key component of the standard toolbox held by technical experts, and the way they usually work is by applying existing knowledge specifically to matters of efficiency and precision, to produce outcomes that are both tangible and measurable. A great example of a technical solution, common throughout the trust industry, is implementing new trust accounting technology.

Adaptive solutions are different in that they focus on fixing the person (or organization) having the problem. Adaptive solutions take into account that the source of the challenge lies within the person and their values, beliefs, and behaviors. Adaptive solutions often deal with Invisible Threats that are assumed or believed to be facts. They focus on individual growth, where the person has to learn the way forward. But the individuals themselves can't see this because of their blind spots, so they often try to use technical solutions to achieve an adaptive result, which doesn't work.

These two approaches, technical and adaptive, require not only different skillsets but different mindsets. If you're seeking external help for an adaptive solution, by definition this means the solution is going to entail learning and potentially having to adapt yourself, or your organization, to a completely different point of view or way of seeing your environment. In other words, you need an adaptive solution to make your blind spots visible.

To be clear, a technical solution can sometimes be just the ticket for fixing the problem you have. But only when the problem is clearly understood and the solution well known. Moreover, a technical solution is often applicable but only as part of the fix, not the entire solution needed. In either case—when the problem and solution are unknown or when the technical solution is only part of the fix needed—you need to beware. This is where things can get messy.

Understandably, professional fiduciary firms, like any other organization, have a tendency to look for the quick fix. And sometimes a quick fix is indeed possible, but again, only if the challenges they're dealing with are well known—for example, the kind where a standard technical solution, one right out of a consultant's inventory, is generally sufficient for the job at hand.

Often, however, this is just wishful thinking, as what the organization really needs is an approach that can identify internal contradictions in values, beliefs, and behaviors, and brings to the surface the causes of those contradictions.

There are no technical solutions that can do that. But the wishful thinking prevails.

AN INTERVENTION THAT MADE ALL THE DIFFERENCE

Jeff was *trying* to get the right help for his problem. What was his problem? Jeff believed he had a great business idea. He wanted to establish a de novo trust company and had taken steps to get this off the ground, including locating a great office space and leasing it on the spot for a five-year term. The space was large enough for a staff of twelve, with a great conference room for board and client meetings that had fabulous mountain views. On top of that, Jeff had hired a law firm to put together the necessary application to the state. Jeff's only missing piece was the capital. He had raised some funds, but not enough.

So Jeff hired a consulting firm, who recommended he hire one of their picks for a Board Chair, an individual who would help identify investors with deep pockets to bring in that capital. This Board Chair was very high-priced and, after Jeff agreed to engage him, got right down to business, quickly organizing a get-together with everyone who was already on the new company's team at the new office location. Prospective investors were also invited but only a few attended the investor meetings. Ultimately, none were interested in investing the millions needed for the de novo trust company.

Still, Jeff believed in his business idea and knew it was a great one. In his mind, the only piece of the puzzle that his new business organization was missing was the de novo trust company, with a trust license to allow them to handle estate planning and investment management services for their clients on the front end, and estate administration and asset transfers to the next generation on the back end, after the death of those clients many years later.

Despite hiring the recommended Board Chair, however, nothing seemed to be going as planned. The following year brought nothing but frustration for Jeff. He dutifully went along with all of the Board Chair's instructions: created decks and video clips; hosted small groups of prospective investors, both at the new office space as well as his organization's home state office location; cold-called people on lists of angel investors (also provided, by the way, through the same consulting firm who'd first recommended the Board Chair); and even changed up his casual business attire to include a button-down shirt and tie, as he'd been exhorted to do by the Board Chair, in the event a hasty virtual meeting with a prospective investor suddenly cropped up. So far, they had gotten only small investments, not nearly enough to capitalize the de novo trust company. As fast as these small investments came into the fledgling company, the money was spent on consulting fees, rent, and salaries, including a hefty one for the Board Chair. Simply put, Jeff and his original business partners were making no headway in getting the millions needed to start the trust company, which was the essential missing piece in their ambitious plan.

Jeff believed so strongly in his idea that he'd poured not only all his time into it but also his own money. His wife, Renée, who was his biggest supporter, even agreed, willingly, to downsize their home and make other financial sacrifices. She also helped the company with branding and design work, coming up with an amazing logo for the de novo trust company.

That spring, the Board Chair requested another team meeting. Agendas were drafted, then scrapped and completely revised by the Board Chair. Travel plans were made for everyone on the team, including those who had been at that first meeting the year before in the new office location and those who had been brought on since. This time, the meeting would last a full week and would be held at Jeff's other company's home state location. It would also feature an outside consultant (from another consulting firm Jeff had used in the past) to help with the required trust company-specific de novo application documentation—a purely technical solution that was nonetheless a necessary component to accompany the application for the trust license. Jeff thought that the outside consultant, who had seemed very knowledgeable on technical trust-specific matters, might be helpful to have around if trust company-specific questions cropped up during the week.

Over the first few days of meetings, the Board Chair shared

many great ideas, all geared toward how the new company would operate once it had its trust license and, more urgently, what the new presentation deck should look like in order to attract a major potential investor.

But the Board Chair was also doing something not so great: sowing seeds of discontent. As an example, the developer and sole owner of the estate planning software (who was key to the entire business plan) was brought in, only to be told in front of everyone in the meeting that the Board Chair thought the new company should just buy the software outright. But for the software creator, this was his baby, and he was not willing to part with it. He just got up and abruptly left the meeting to head back home. Some of the other people who had been brought in to help—such as the photographer hired to take pictures for the website, and the chief investment officer of an institutional RIA firm that would be providing the investment management services for the trust assets—also seemed put off by the Board Chair's manner.

What was really going on under the surface? The truth of the matter, outrageous at it may seem, was that the Board Chair appeared to be trying to take over Jeff's business plan and ideas.

At the end of the weeklong meeting, almost everyone headed to the airport and their homes. Except for the outside consultant. The Board Chair had instructed him to stay on an extra week—at Jeff's expense, no less—to make sure the presentation deck included the necessary trust technical information and would be ready to go. In the meantime, rather than linger in town for the weekend, the consultant ventured out on a road trip to a nearby city. He needed to clear his head and think through the events of the previous week. He'd found the entire experience unsettling, to say the least. By the next day, a Saturday, the consultant's concerns had only grown more pronounced. So, he decided to call

Jeff and suggest meeting up for dinner the following evening. He asked Jeff to bring along his wife, Renée, as well.

It was during that Sunday dinner that Jeff got the help he needed. The right help.

Like the consultant, Jeff's head had been spinning after the week of meetings facilitated by the Board Chair. He couldn't shake the feeling that something was off and was still in this agitated state of mind when the three sat down for dinner. Then, his worst fears were confirmed. Even before having a chance to open the menus, the consultant looked directly across the table at Jeff and Renée and told them flat-out that they needed to take action to protect their business or they would lose it. He warned Jeff that the interests of the Board Chair were not at all aligned with what Jeff wanted to accomplish. He also told Jeff that he suspected the Board Chair was fomenting discontent among the team, especially among the biggest investors to date, Jeff's very own original business partners.

That was when something shifted in Jeff. It was as if he saw a lifeline. He was hearing the things he needed to hear, and from a trusted person, someone neutral who had nothing to gain from putting this idea into his head. The consultant was motivating Jeff to take action, the same way Mom Florez had motivated Matt decades earlier. Jeff then turned to his wife and saw her nodding her head in agreement with the consultant's words. As it turns out, Renée had been sensing the same bad vibes from the Board Chair but had been hesitant to say anything to Jeff because he'd seemed so excited about having this guy on the Board.

As for the consultant, now that he saw he had Jeff's attention, and Renée's support, he proceeded to lay out a path for Jeff's new company. It was a path that did not require being told what to do or how to do it by the Board Chair, who seemed less intent on helping Jeff raise the necessary capital for the de novo trust company than on taking from Jeff's business idea as much as he could, whether in the form of his large salary, expenses for travel, or, worse—namely convincing those one or two serious investors Jeff *had* managed to locate to instead invest in other business ventures the Board Chair had his personal funds invested in.

That Sunday evening at dinner, the outside consultant also helped sow the initial seeds in Jeff's mind that he, Jeff, could do this business his *own* way, the successful way he'd used in the past to achieve success in his first business. What's more, Jeff saw that his wife, who he now understood had her own reservations about the Board Chair, continued to believe unwaveringly not only in Jeff's business idea but also his ability to succeed on his own.

Did the outside consultant's advice work? Was it the right help?

Let's look at what happened next. A few months later, the Board Chair engineered a coup to get the Board to fire the CFO, who had been Jeff's faithful business partner in his original business as well as in the new venture. Over the years, this was someone who had also become Jeff's friend, and now the recent turn of events had left Jeff understandably shaken. But he recalled what the outside consultant had told him at their dinner. Gradually, Jeff was starting to see that he didn't need to stay on the path the Board Chair was trying to engineer—a path that seemed to be spiraling down and out of control.

So he decided to take action, and a few weeks later, took the bold step himself of firing the Board Chair, despite the threat of being sued. As you may guess, Jeff's very next step was rehiring his CFO!

After this, Jeff was reenergized and motivated to continue

down the business path he had first set in motion, the same path he had initially envisioned for his business.

Just as Mom Florez had done for Matt, the outside consultant had given Jeff the kick he needed at that Sunday dinner by recognizing, and sharing with Jeff, what he really needed to do when he couldn't see it himself. It took that kick for Jeff to see he had to change his mindset. In this way, the outside consultant certainly turned out to be "the right help" for Jeff. Because of the consultant's intervention during the dinner, ultimately Jeff was able to take the inspiration it sparked in him to adapt. Moreover, Jeff did this by shifting his lens to believe that yes, he and Renée could and should hang onto the business idea and not dilute ownership. And yes, Jeff could and should continue on his path and not let someone who didn't have his best interests in mind dictate what he should do or how he should do it.

But until that fateful dinner where the consultant inspired him, Jeff wouldn't have been able to imagine let alone pull off the big shakeup that needed to take place. Even after this important intervention, Jeff wasn't 100 percent sure he had what it took to fix the situation. It was only when the Board—at the instigation of the Board Chair—voted to fire Jeff's beloved CFO that he remembered the outside consultant's words and vowed to turn the tide, fire the Board Chair, and re-hire the CFO. As he hatched his plan, Jeff even took to calling the consultant for moral support and ongoing encouragement.

It worked. Jeff ended up not only regaining total control of his company but reclaiming his true path. He was proud of himself.

ADAPTIVE WORK AVOIDANCE

One might think that an unsatisfying outcome from a technical solution or a series of technical solutions—like what happened with Jeff when he hired a firm to find angel investors and they instead recommended he hire their pick for a Board Chair—would be enough to give a person pause and compel them to reconsider their approach. Instead, what often happens is the person just attempts a different technical solution to solve whatever new symptoms have emerged.

We have seen this pattern repeat itself over and over, for years in some organizations, often to the tune of hundreds of thousands, if not millions, of dollars spent to apply technical solutions that never seem to work or that work just for a short time.

Why, one might wonder, would an organization's management put up with this?

Here's how we see it from the consultant side of things. It's not that management are burying their faces in the sand. They know that changes need to happen in order to solve their problems and close the gap between expectations and reality. That's why they pick the third option of the standard business decision-tree: instead of doing nothing or just trying to lower expectations, they endeavor to change their current reality by solving the specific problems their organization faces.

But here's the rub: management is still not doing the adaptive work they need to. They haven't yet accepted and embraced the 3′ Prime solution that calls for not just any kind of change but adaptive change. In fact, what they're really engaging in is something we term *adaptive work avoidance*. This is a pattern we've seen repeated at numerous organizations. But it's not because management or staff are unwilling to make an effort or work hard toward effecting change. Oftentimes it's quite the opposite: organizations that have exhausted themselves with changes wrought by the seemingly endless string of technical solutions that either don't work or don't work for long.

Granted, the adaptive work avoidance we observe in so many organizations is occasionally rooted in a true reluctance to adapt. More often, however, the avoidance stems from an inability to see what adaptive change is needed.

In the Jeff story, the outside consultant recognized fairly early on that Jeff—in trying to solve his problem of bringing in the necessary investment capital for his new business—was still thinking he could rely on technical solutions like hiring other people, namely a Board Chair. Jeff had become adept at adaptive work avoidance, assuming that in order to get big investors, he needed to hire high-priced help.

But the outside consultant then motivated Jeff by explaining that he not only could, but should, wrest control of his company back from the Board Chair he'd hired. The outside consultant also helped Jeff see that he could, and in fact should, be the one to raise the necessary investment capital for his business idea.

Another reason Jeff had been avoiding the adaptive work (that he ultimately recognized he needed to do) was, frankly, he feared he might fail in raising the funds to get the de novo trust company off the ground. It was the outside consultant who helped Jeff change his mindset. He inspired Jeff to face his fears head on, believe in himself again, and get rid of anything and anyone standing in the way of his moving forward with his business idea.

Then, after the Board voted off the CFO, Jeff adapted. His mindset shift—to believing in himself—helped him finally see that *he* needed to be the one running the show: it was his idea, his passion, and his belief in the business that gave the best chance for success.

Why did it take so long to get to this realization? Why is adaptive work avoidance so prevalent, not just in professional fiduciary firms but across organizations in all fields of business? Well, there's no getting around it: true adaptive change is hard. It demands much more than hiring consultants or getting high-priced board members. It's about changing underlying value systems.

ADAPTIVE CHANGE IS ABOUT CHANGING THE PERSON WITH THE PROBLEM—COULD THAT BE YOU?

To achieve adaptive success, you and others in your firm must be open to systemic change and cultivating resilience—longer-term solutions—so that future changes to the underlying environment or additional complexities won't throw you off the right path.

Among the professional fiduciary firms we've worked with, unfortunately we've seen some that will do anything to avoid having to engage in this kind of adaptive work. They'll fight it to the bitter end. And we mean that literally. Desperate to buy themselves more time, they'll keep hiring help to implement technical solutions, only to learn it was not the right help, or will ignore the right help that is being proffered, until eventually they go out of business.

When we talk about the Invisible Threat, this is a big part of what we mean. If the term sounds menacing, that's because it's meant to. Adaptive work avoidance puts professional fiduciary firms, and the people who work at those firms, at risk. It's the risk of not seeing the Invisible Threats along their path because of hidden assumptions and beliefs preventing them from undertaking the 3′ Prime Option, i.e., adaptive change.

Don't become another casualty. Get the right help. Be willing to embrace, not avoid, adaptive work. This is just the beginning. Embracing adaptive work and eliminating blind spots will require you to cross a threshold—a process we call *entering the gate*.

GETTING THE RIGHT HELP

1. FIXING SYMPTOMS VS. CHALLENGING UNDERLYING ASSUMPTIONS

Standard Approach and Outcome:
- Focus on fixing visible symptoms of problems (e.g., engaging Board Chair to help raise capital).
- Example: Jeff's initial actions, like hiring expensive Board Chair and assuming he would bring in needed capital, did not address core issue stemming from hidden assumption about Jeff's own capabilities.
- Outcome: Temporary fix of one issue, Board Chair in place, but persistent underlying problems when this high-priced fix does not bring in needed capital.

Counterintuitive Approach and Expected Outcome:
- Challenge hidden assumptions and change mindset.
- Example: Jeff recognizes need to change his mindset and approach to raising capital.
- Expected Outcome: Sustainable, long-term solution that resolves root causes.

2. TECHNICAL SOLUTIONS VS. ADAPTIVE SOLUTIONS

Standard Approach and Outcome:

- Rely on technical solutions (e.g., new technology, external consultants) for all problems.
- Example: Jeff hired consultants and high-priced Board Chair to attract investors, because these technical solutions were intuitive and made logical sense at the time.
- Outcome: Short-term fixes that do not address deeper issues.

Counterintuitive Approach and Expected Outcome:

- Embrace adaptive solutions that focus on changing the person and their values, beliefs, and behaviors.
- Example: Jeff's reliance on technical solutions, such as hiring consultants and a Board Chair, failed to secure funding. When Jeff changes his mindset and regains control of his business he makes progress.
- Expected Outcome: Deeper understanding and long-term resolution of problems.

3. SEEKING THE RIGHT HELP

Standard Approach and Outcome:

- Seek quick fixes and assume external help will solve all problems.
- Example: Jeff repeatedly sought external consultants without achieving his goal of securing major investment.
- Outcome: Continued struggles and reliance on ineffective solutions.

Counterintuitive Approach and Expected Outcome:

- Seek the right help that challenges your hidden assumptions and promotes adaptive change.
- Example: Jeff's repeated attempts to get quick fixes from external consultants worked once he found the right help that challenged his hidden assumptions and guided him towards adaptive change.
- Expected Outcome: Effective problem-solving and sustainable growth.

CHAPTER 3

ENTERING THE GATE

WHEN A TRUST ORGANIZATION FACES ONGOING CHAL-lenges or exceptions to policy, the industry norm is to escalate these issues up the chain of command. First, management passes the problem to a committee. If that doesn't resolve it, it goes to the Board of Directors. According to trust company regulations and supervisory expectations, the Board is ultimately responsible for oversight of the trust company's day-to-day execution of its fiduciary powers through its senior officers, management, trust officers, and supporting control functions. Essentially, these groups act as gatekeepers for a professional fiduciary firm. The Board and its committees adopt policies and have oversight of its fiduciary activities. Management, including its committees, execute those policies through procedures, processes, and systems, and provide appropriate Board and committee reporting to support their oversight responsibilities.

Before the GLBA was passed in 1999, trust departments within commercial banks had well-established oversight, governance structures, policies, procedures, processes, and systems in place for dealing with trust department problems. Even when issues were escalated to a committee or the Board, they were handled using standard *technical* solutions by professional fiduciaries who knew their stuff. This system worked because Board members and management had years of experience and the right fiduciary knowledge to make the appropriate decisions.

However, with the GLBA and the increased entry of financial firms into diverse business combinations, new invisible threats emerged. For organizations new to the trust business, many of these problems were unlike anything they'd seen before. The environment for trust administration shifted dramatically from a straightforward bank trust department or standalone trust company to a complex wealth management industry involving affiliated "banking" (e.g., trust companies) and nonbanking entities (e.g., SEC registered broker-dealers and investment advisors). The result of all these developments is that, in today's complex wealth management industry, problems that crop up and cause stress are not being resolved. The traditional methods and dependencies are simply no longer effective—they are way too siloed, as are their different US regulators.

Professional fiduciary firms now operate in an entirely new domain and must adapt in order to "enter the gate" and navigate this modern trust landscape. But true adaptive change requires more than just expanding one's skills and knowledge. As we mentioned in Chapter 2, adaptive change means changing *you*. For such change to take place, there must be a letting-go—letting go of what you know, your assumptions and beliefs—and a willingness to accept that your current knowledge and skills are insufficient to close the gap. Those are what drove the solutions you've already tried. The ones that didn't work. True adaptive change requires an acceptance that you've reached the limit of your knowledge. Even more important, it requires faith—in others, in a higher power, and in the fact that (whatever form it may take) adaptive change is what's needed to close the gap between what you want and what you have.

The letting-go is the acknowledgment you've reached the limit of your knowledge and abilities. It is the *new* assumption, the belief that adaptive change is not only possible but necessary to achieve your goals. We refer to this as *entering the gate*, and it means that not only you and your team but your whole professional fiduciary firm—including Board members, management, and committee members—must also be willing to let go of what they know as they take on new roles as wealth management gatekeepers. Their responsibility is to ensure that fiduciary powers are exercised with the right amount of prudence and care, using an appropriate fiduciary lens. This will be a completely different approach from what they've done in the past.

For example, imagine a bank trust department that formerly dealt primarily with trust administration and investment management services. After GLBA, their Board decides to expand their business offerings to include brokerage services through an affiliated broker-dealer. The bank has, in effect, expanded their services and are, for all intents and purposes, now in the "wealth management" business. But have they actually entered the gate of wealth management? Probably not. They still need to understand and navigate the complexities of brokerage regulations and practices. Moreover, they need to do all this while continuing to stay on top of the ongoing complexities of the trust services they provide. And, of course, they need to keep these two businesses—the trust and brokerage operations—appropriately segregated, so that conflict-of-interest and self-dealing exposure don't skyrocket!

Just diversifying its business lines to provide wealth management services does *not* mean the bank has made the adaptive change necessary to achieve its goals.

We can't stress this enough: moving into other financial businesses requires professional fiduciary firms and their Boards to adapt and expand their expertise beyond the traditional bank trust department of yesteryear. Entering the gate of wealth management is a transition that demands an awareness of the adaptive challenge ahead (i.e., the letting-go). This is how you build the deep understanding of what it means to combine all these different people, regulations, practices, cultures, and challenges to effectively fulfill fiduciary duties within the broader wealth management industry.

Entering the gate of wealth management is no different than how we all, from time to time, face our own personal gates where, in order to achieve our goals, we must let go of what we know and envision a different possibility for ourselves. Take, for example, the story of Matt's lifestyle change. He struggled with weight loss for most of his life, trying numerous diets and exercise routines, but nothing had worked in the long term. It wasn't until he was willing to let go of his assumptions and beliefs to enter the gate of an adaptive lifestyle change that he began to see real progress and the hope of long-term success.

ENTERING THE GATE TO A HEALTHIER LIFE

MATT: As you'll remember from Chapter 1, I was only ten when my mom was diagnosed with cancer. Then, over the next three years, and especially toward the end of that difficult period, I felt like I was losing her bit by bit as she struggled in her brave fight against the disease. Meanwhile, my father was struggling to pay the medical bills and support our family. It was a very tough time, and it deeply affected my siblings and me, even if I didn't have the words as a young boy to describe it.

But this challenging phase also marked the beginning of

a different kind of struggle in my life, one that I haven't mentioned yet. I'm talking about my lifelong battle with weight and weight management. Before my mom got sick, I was a pretty thin kid. For one thing, I was very physically active, as children tended to be in those days, before computers and smart phones came on the scene. I was always out and about in the neighborhood, running around and playing games with the other kids on the block.

As for what I ate, well it was basically whatever my mom put on the table. She cooked all our meals and kept us healthy and well-fed. But after she became sick and especially when she started having to be in the hospital so much, our eating patterns changed. Our budget also shrank. Cheap, processed foods, often donated by friends trying to lend a hand, became my norm. So much so that, even after my mom passed, I couldn't let go of those starchy comfort foods, sugary sodas, and the like.

As a teenager, I gained a lot of weight. There are photos from that time, like one with me and my baseball team, where I definitely stand out as the chubby kid in the picture. But it was nothing compared to how big I became in my twenties and thirties and beyond. The weight just kept piling on, even after I made my way in the world and could afford to eat better. I was still addicted to those same unhealthy foods that had infiltrated my diet as a young boy: pizza, soda, fast food.

At the height of my weight gain, I was almost 300 pounds—in a five-foot-seven frame. I couldn't fit into clothing, couldn't fit into airplane seats. It definitely affected my lifestyle and took a toll on not just me but my loved ones. In fact, it was largely due to Joanne and our son Ben's encouragement that at age fifty-seven, I was finally able to adapt, almost half a century after first picking up those bad eating habits.

That was when I entered the gate to a healthier life.

But I'm getting ahead of myself. Remember, this wasn't the first time I had tried to lose weight. In fact, I had been through a few earlier cycles of losing thirty pounds and gaining it all back again. Joanne and I had even started going to Weight Watchers together six years earlier and both lost thirty pounds. Of course I then made the classic mistake, or invalid assumption, of believing I was cured and soon gained back those thirty and then some. You see, I had never really adapted. My mindset never changed. So, naturally, I reverted to the same person I'd always been—the all-too-familiar chubby kid staring at me from an old photograph.

It wasn't until June of 2009 that something clicked for me. We were at a Saturday morning Weight Watchers meeting where one of the other members was being recognized for having lost over one hundred pounds. It made me wonder whether I was capable of such a dramatic change. I knew I could lose thirty. In fact, I had become kind of an expert at it since I'd been losing and re-gaining those thirty (and more) pounds more times than I cared to admit.

What would it even take, I wondered, for me to lose one hundred pounds? I would have to essentially change who I was. The Weight Watchers mantra was all about "eating better," not eating less. But up to this point, I had only kind of paid attention to the philosophy, the principles behind the program. I had just assumed that the message was the same diet mentality I'd always latched onto when trying to lose weight. Over my many years of struggling with weight loss, I had internalized this mentality: just eat less and you'll lose the weight. At that meeting, though, I started to wonder. If I wanted to lose one hundred pounds—and even more importantly, if I wanted to keep it off—would I have to change who I was? Was the problem me? If I could adapt, change who I was, could I perhaps become the kind of person who could lose, and keep off, one hundred pounds?

I remember listening to that Weight Watchers member talk about her weight loss journey and trying to visualize myself in her position, picturing myself as someone who had already lost the weight and was just casually talking about it in a meeting. It seemed scary. The member talked about all the adaptive changes she'd made in her life, even ending long-time relationships with her so-called friends who she used to indulge with in her former habits and now consistently tried to sabotage her lifestyle change. Yet, I also felt a glimmer of hope that Saturday morning. It was faint at first but definitely there: a positive sensation that arose from my visualizing what I might look like in the future, one hundred pounds lighter. I also saw the dangers, however, associated with the complexity and uncertainty that went along with adapting—changing who I was.

At our meeting the next Saturday, the same member, the one who had lost all the weight, walked into the room and I was just bowled over by her confidence. It was then I started to believe I might actually be able to do this: enter the same gate as her and lose one hundred pounds. So, I decided at that very moment I was really going to do it. I was willing to let go of what I knew about weight loss—that diet mentality—and also willing to admit I had been holding an invalid assumption that losing thirty pounds meant I was "cured" and could return to old habits. It felt good. But I still wasn't sure what was supposed to come next. All I knew was that I'd entered a new gate in my life and was on my path to a healthier lifestyle.

The next assumption I had to challenge was one I'd held for as long as I could remember. I'm talking about my assumption around what food is. In my mind, food was what I was fed. I just ate what I ate; I didn't find it necessary to make decisions about it. Perhaps because of this long-held assumption, I also didn't have any knowledge about eating better.

I had also assumed that my weight issues were a matter of genetics, and therefore largely out of my control. I looked like my father did, and like his father had looked before he died. We Eby men were pear-shaped; it just ran in our family. You can't change biology. Or so I believed.

But these weren't the only assumptions I had to challenge. When it came to my relationship with food, I'd just always assumed that it was normal to eat to celebrate, or to use food as a tool for emotional management, whether anger, sadness, or joy. I had an all-or-nothing belief about how to lose weight: eat and gain weight, or don't eat and lose weight. It was a fixed mindset—a conviction without proof—that had led to many years of yo-yo dieting.

Finally, there was the belief that because I'd always been overweight, I could not change.

Flash forward to today: it's been over twelve years since I lost those one hundred pounds and I'm happy to report I've succeeded in keeping them off. Not only do I eat better; I also exercise regularly. When I meet new people these days, they just assume I've always been this size; and, if they find out about my weight loss, they can't seem to believe it, even when I show them a "before" photo. In many ways, I feel like a completely different person—and then I realize that, in fact, I am!

STEPPING INTO THE UNKNOWN

As a professional fiduciary firm in today's wealth management industry you may be essentially in the same spot Matt was when he went from feeling forever stuck in the lose thirty/gain thirty mindset to entering the gate to a new path forward and believing he was capable of adaptive change. You are at the point where you must decide whether to enter the gate, be willing to *let go*, and step into the unknown.

In Matt's case, embracing the adaptive challenge of life-changing weight loss made him feel empowered rather than afraid of the unknown after he entered the gate to a healthier life, despite the uncertainties ahead.

This willingness to accept the unknown represents a crucial mind shift, and one you must internalize as you consider your own adaptive challenges you'll face once you enter the gate. To be successful, you have to be willing to let go of what you know and accept the uncertainties on the other side. In particular, you have to accept that with adaptive change, there may be no "right" answers. In fact, you can bet on it.

Entering the gate is the pivotal moment when you confront your blind spots, challenge your old assumptions and beliefs, and yes, step into the unknown. It is the threshold of transformation, where the path to adaptive success begins to unfold. We saw that happen many years ago with a very well-intentioned small bank trust department that had gotten stuck in their struggles to help beneficiaries of special needs trusts. The department was so small it had just a single trust officer. For the purposes of this story, we'll call her Mary, and to better preserve the anonymity of that trust department and trust officer, we'll give her the persona of an individual certified public accountant (CPA) acting on her own as she entered the gate to a new path forward—a career as a professional fiduciary.

HOW MARY ENTERED THE GATE

Mary, a skilled CPA, had been tasked with completing a number of US Income Tax Returns for Estates and Trusts (Form 1041) for special, or supplemental, needs trusts (commonly referred to in the industry simply as SNTs). It was the first time she had completed 1041s for SNTs—the opportunity came her way after she had worked on the corporate tax returns for a non-profit business that provided housing and education for special needs individuals. The CEO of this non-profit was so pleased with her work that he asked whether he could hand out her business card to special needs families.

Mary enjoyed the SNT work, not because completing 1041s for special needs trusts was so very exciting or different from regular 1041s for other types of irrevocable trusts, but because she had gotten to know the parents of the special needs individuals. She had also learned about the many specific challenges of working with SNTs. In fact, because of these challenges, it seemed there were few professionals in her industry willing to accept the responsibilities associated with being professional fiduciaries for SNTs.

At first, Mary was the same way. She didn't want to get into the SNT world. But then the parents of one particular special needs individual pleaded with her to help them. The parents were aging and they had no other family to help with the trust. How could Mary say no? Before she knew it, she had agreed to accept an appointment as the trustee for that SNT.

As a CPA, Mary already had the requisite professional mindset and trustworthiness, which was one of the reasons these parents had reached out to her in the first place. And the work seemed simple enough, at least for that first year. As the successor trustee, Mary took over the responsibility of a bank account where the monthly disability checks for the special needs individual were deposited, and then ensured that payments for the services provided for the beneficiary were made on time.

Completing the 1041 for that SNT the next tax season also

turned out to be quite simple for Mary. She already had access to all the financial information needed to complete the return. So, when another set of parents approached her to take on the trusteeship for their special needs child, Mary willingly agreed. From there, before she knew it, she had two dozen SNTs for which she served as trustee!

But when she accepted the professional fiduciary responsibilities for all those other SNTs, Mary had taken on more than she realized. Yes, that very first SNT had been simple. It involved only one bank account to receive monthly disability checks and make a few payments for services provided to the special needs individual. When she accepted trusteeship of the other SNTs, Mary assumed that all SNTs were equally simple: receive government funds, make necessary payments, and complete the 1041s each year. Mary assumed there was no real decision-making involved. She didn't have the experience to know her blind spots when it came to administering SNTs, and her hidden assumptions prevented her from seeing them.

Mary administered the trustee duties for the SNTs with her usual professional skills. It was not until the next tax season, while preparing the 1041s for the SNTs, that some problems appeared. She had sent money directly to some of the SNT beneficiaries, and when completing the tax returns for those SNTs, had started to get concerned. By sending money directly to those special needs individuals, she had inadvertently caused these beneficiaries to receive income. And as a CPA, Mary knew, based on the amount of income they had received, they would need to file personal 1040 tax returns.

Rather than try to explain the problem to the parents, Mary just went ahead and prepared and filed personal tax returns for the ten special needs individuals who had received the income. She gave copies of the trust tax returns, along with the personal returns, to all the parents. But on the invoices she sent them for her tax and trustee services, Mary decided not to include her fees for the preparation of the personal returns. She thought that was the right thing to do, as it was her error in sending money directly to the special needs beneficiaries that caused the need to file personal 1040 tax returns. Mary also decided that she would try her best not to send money directly to the special needs beneficiaries in the future, even if asked by their parents to do so, given that it had created a personal tax issue. At this point, Mary assumed her mistake in sending those funds directly to the beneficiaries was merely a tax matter.

As trustee of the SNTs, Mary had begun receiving a lot of mail, not only from the banks that held SNT money in checking accounts, but from various government agencies, including the IRS. Mary also noticed other mail that had drifted in. As a CPA, she recognized she was receiving tax reports from various entities that seemed related to the SNTs, but she was not quite sure how. Only after tax season was over that April, did Mary decide to look more closely at some of those tax reports. First, she organized everything, as was her wont, into various piles, then labelled some file folders, put the tax reports into them, and spread the folders out on her desk.

Upon closer inspection, Mary grew concerned and realized she would have to amend more than one of the trust 1041 tax returns she had just filed. The tax reports sent from various entities clearly indicated that most of the SNTs she was trustee for owned more than just the bank checking accounts she'd assumed were the only assets in those trusts. She saw 1099 forms from brokerage firms that showed some trusts owned brokerage accounts, which had generated income and realized capital gains. There were K-1s from business entities also owned by the SNTs that showed revenue or losses that would have to be reported. She also saw more than a few 1099R reports from custody accounts that showed distributions coming out of inherited retirement accounts being sent directly to the special needs beneficiaries, which she realized was problematic. All this mail revealed huge tax issues for the SNTs Mary had just filed the 1041s for—incorrect filings that would have to be amended, with accompanying IRS penalties and interest. *What a disaster*, Mary thought to herself.

She got right to work amending those ten trust tax returns for the SNTs. A few days later, when Mary submitted the last of the amended returns, she breathed a sigh of relief and left town for a well-deserved vacation in the Bahamas. She assumed all the problems were resolved and enjoyed her time away. What she couldn't see—because of the blind spots she had when it came to administering SNTs—was that as she relaxed poolside sipping Piña Coladas, even more alarming invisible threats hidden in those SNTs awaited her back home. She was about to discover that being trustee of SNTs was far more challenging than she could ever have imagined.

When she got home from vacation and saw the pile of mail stacked just inside her front door, Mary just dumped it into a box and shoved it into the back of a closet, planning to go through it later that week. The next afternoon, while working in her home office getting caught up on emails, Mary's doorbell started chiming, not just once but over and over again. "What on earth?" she muttered as she got up to see what could be so urgent. It was the postman, so she opened the door, only to be handed a huge post office box filled to the brim with mail—all for her!

After closing the door, she fumbled around with the box to get a better grip on it and lugged it into her dining room. There she dumped it out and realized it was all, every last envelope, related to those darn SNTs. She ran to the closet where she'd shoved the other mail, and dumped all that mail on the table too. She started to open envelopes at random, and it all seemed bad. Account statements for assets she didn't know existed. Tax notices for incorrect returns with penalties and interest accruing every day. But worse than anything were the letters from government agencies notifying her of their intention to cut off various disability payments (Medicaid and other government services) because the special needs individuals earnings had exceeded their income cap the previous year—all because Mary had mistakenly sent funds directly to them.

At this point, Mary wondered why she had ever accepted this business in the first place. In her career as a CPA, she'd never done any professional fiduciary work whatsoever, never mind taking on the two-dozen SNTs she had been so excited about. What had she been thinking? She'd assumed she was doing good by helping out the parents and taking over the trustee duties from them. But now she was overcome with guilt and regret, and couldn't sleep that night, agonizing over thoughts of something even worse going wrong.

She woke up very early the next morning and started to do online research about administering SNTs. Mary assumed that with a little digging she could figure out what her duties as a professional fiduciary were supposed to be, then just go back and fix everything. But the more she read about the subject, the more she realized how little she actually knew about being trustee of SNTs. What a dilemma! Mary couldn't just walk away. She couldn't stick all that mail back in the closet and put her blinders back on. More than even the risk to her as a professional CPA and as a trustee, Mary was concerned about the beneficiaries of the SNTs. She had no idea how to fix things, and was horrified by the very real harm she'd already caused to those trusting parents and beneficiaries.

Less than a week later, Mary sat in a class she had signed up for after coming across it while researching how to administer SNTs. She wasn't sure she made the right decision to attend, thinking it might be a waste of time. She knew she'd have twice as much work piled up when she got back to her office and felt hopeless anyway—how could a class give her all she needed to solve problems she didn't fully grasp? When the instructor began to speak, though, Mary's ears perked up. That first day, she listened in growing horror, realizing she'd approached administration of SNTs in the wrong way from the very beginning. But by the second day of class, she felt a glimmer of hope as the instructor laid out the path to successful administration of SNTs.

The class was indeed helpful. On the one hand, Mary already realized it wouldn't get her nearly as far as she needed to fix everything she'd messed up. But on the other, she also started to see a path forward. She paid attention to the instructor's every word, and learned SNTs were a unique type of trust and the journey to being able to skillfully administer them was long and challenging. To compound the complexity, Mary learned that federal and state laws that governed SNTs and public assistance programs were ever-changing—trustees of SNTs had to stay current with all that to make sure no benefits were missed and no mistakes were made to cause loss of those benefits.

Despite how daunting it was, Mary remained passionate about being able to help those families whose SNTs she had taken on in the first place. It was noble work and she wanted to learn everything she could about how to become a skilled professional fiduciary, like the others in her class seemed to be. But she had no time to get up to speed. She was already trustee of the trusts, and she'd already messed these up. Now it was her job to ensure they were properly administered going forward, and time was of the essence.

Back when she first accepted the professional fiduciary responsibilities, Mary had assumed that as a CPA she had the professional acumen and tax knowledge required to administer SNTs. She also assumed, after her experience with that first SNT, that they were all the same and she could administer them all in the same way. She assumed that when problems arose at tax time, she could use her CPA experience to fix things—just by preparing the personal tax returns.

By taking the class, Mary was able to challenge her assumptions, which she could see now had been wrong. She'd never had the right fiduciary training, experience, and lens to see the invisible threats of administering SNTs. While she was not yet sure what to do, she knew she had to change who she was and not just her approach to administering SNTs.

She went from feeling like she didn't belong in the class that first day, to trying to visualize herself as a professional fiduciary, confidently administering trusts like those around her. It seemed scary, but that glimmer of hope grew into a sense of what it might feel like to be a successful trustee of SNTs, administering them with confidence and due care for the beneficiaries. Mary also saw the dangers—the problems caused by her mistakes—and the complexity and uncertainty that went along with adapting, changing who she was. After all, she was a CPA. Could she adapt to a be CPA skilled at administering SNTs?

By mid-week, Mary knew she'd gotten the right help by attending this class. Hour by hour, little by little, the fog covering those threats thinned and she started to understand the mistakes she'd made.

During the lunch break on the last day of class, she listened to classmates as they shared some horror stories on issues they'd struggled with but ultimately were able to fix. Mary was so impressed, and not a little humbled, that these people who had been dealing with SNTs for years, who she thought were already experts in SNTs, listened with rapt attention to their instructor explain challenges with recent changes to federal and state laws. Mary recognized she was among a group of seasoned professional fiduciaries, people who knew and understood the trust industry and could successfully navigate the complexities of SNTs. She wondered if they would be able to help her, but feared they might instead report her to the authorities if they learned about all of her missteps to date. (Mary wasn't quite sure who those authorities might be, but feared their ominous knock on her door nonetheless.)

It was through listening to those horror stories at lunch that last day of class that Mary really saw the way forward. She realized that those around her, the ones so expert in SNTs, were once in the same fog that circled around her when it came to administering SNTs.

Mary knew she wanted to remain as the trustee of what she now thought of as *her* SNTs. She'd learned in class that because she had accepted appointment to serve as trustee, she owed duties to those trusts and to the special needs beneficiaries. Mary felt even more passionate now about helping the special needs individuals and their families. She wanted to be able to do all the things required of a professional fiduciary. But she also knew she didn't yet have what it took to be one.

Nonetheless, Mary saw that if she was willing to let go of her assumptions, change how she had approached those SNTs in the past, and accept that there might lurk even more Invisible Threats ahead, she could *enter the gate*, beyond which lay the path toward becoming a true professional fiduciary.

Mary eventually joined in with the storytelling and shared a little of what she'd done wrong and why she'd signed up for the class. She confessed to the group that while she feared she'd mishandled her trustee duties, she was determined to do things right in the future, to take whatever steps necessary to succeed. Her classmates, impressed with Mary's passion for becoming a professional fiduciary for SNTs—a type of trust many professional fiduciary firms avoided—gave her encouragement, advice, and even their contact information (because they knew Mary would need more help when she got home). Almost immediately, Mary felt empowered. She had entered the gate to become a true professional fiduciary of SNTs and knew she had found the right path.

ENTERING THE GATE IS EMPOWERING

We saw how Mary confronted her blind spots around administering SNTs, shed her fear about disclosing the mistakes she had already made, and willed herself to *enter the gate* to adaptive change, despite the uncertainties and complexities ahead. By entering the gate to a new path forward and believing she was capable of adaptive change, Mary was able to get out of her fixed mindset and ultimately succeed as a professional fiduciary.

Just like Matt had carried with him the newfound confidence that he was indeed the kind of person who could not only lose one hundred pounds but shift his mindset, adapt *who* he was, and change his very being, Mary used her new knowledge about the challenges of administering SNTs as fuel, drawing on it to reinforce her belief that she was indeed the kind of person who could adapt herself and be a professional fiduciary.

Having entered the gate, then tasted the fruits of this profound shift in their thinking about how to solve what had become very serious problems for each of them, both Matt and Mary became filled with a new sense of possibility; they each saw that there *was* a way forward. They just needed to be willing to *enter the gate*, despite the unknowns, the Invisible Threats in the fog ahead, before they could fully adapt.

Of course, just entering the gate and stepping into the unknown is not enough. The initial sense of empowerment after entering the gate may bring only illusory hope, as the path forward leads to even greater challenges when people feel like the ground beneath them is always shifting in their new environment.

Just imagine an organization like an RIA, with management and a Board of Directors full of financial experts, combining with a newly acquired traditional trust company that supports SNTs and their beneficiaries. The expectations and responsibilities would shift dramatically. In the past, these RIA financial pros would have focused mainly on investment management, using trust powers as a sort of wrapper for their investment services. But as challenging as it is for an RIA to combine with a trust company, combining with a traditional trust company that specializes in SNTs introduces a whole new level of complexity and accountability.

First off, management and the Board would have to expand their focus beyond just running the money. They would need to deeply understand the unique needs and regulations governing SNTs. This means getting up to speed on the ins and outs of administering trusts for special needs beneficiaries, including the crucial task of maintaining their eligibility for government benefits like Medicaid and Social Security. This is not just about knowing the programs; it's about mastering how to navigate them effectively—especially knowing what *not* to do to prevent losing government benefits.

Additionally, management and the Board would have to develop new policies and procedures to ensure trust funds are used appropriately. Establishing strong compliance frameworks would be essential to keep up with the ever-changing landscape of federal and state regulations related to SNTs.

In this new combined business construct, expectations for management and the Board would shift from just overseeing investment strategies to becoming true stewards of the special needs beneficiaries' well-being. They would need to ensure that trust assets are managed wisely, that beneficiaries receive the support and services they need, without making missteps that would jeopardize government benefits, and that the trust's purpose is fulfilled in line with fiduciary duties.

In short, combining a securities firm like an RIA or brokerage firm with a traditional trust company specializing in SNTs would mean a significant shift in expectations and responsibilities for management and the Board of Directors. They would need to adapt and become dedicated fiduciaries focused on the well-being of their beneficiaries. While challenging, this shift in mindset can lead to a more comprehensive and effective approach to wealth management, ensuring that the needs of special needs beneficiaries, who rely in a deep and abiding way on the expertise of those in a position to help them, are met with the utmost care and diligence.

Whew! If it seems like entering the gate of wealth management requires a lot of tradeoffs, well that's because it does. How can you make it a "win-win solution every time"?

ENTERING THE GATE

1. ESCALATION OF ISSUES VS. EXPANDING SKILLS AND KNOWLEDGE

Standard Approach and Outcome:

- Escalate issues to higher levels of authority for resolution.
- Example: Traditionally, trust companies would escalate problems to their Board, expecting Board members to solve known issues using routine procedures.
- Outcome: Resolution through established policies and procedures.

Counterintuitive Approach and Expected Outcome:

- Expand skills and knowledge to navigate new, complex environments.
- Example: Professional fiduciary firms let go of what they know to enter gate into today's wealth management industry.
- Expected Outcome: Process of *letting go* is mindset shift needed to embrace adaptive challenges ahead.

2. TECHNICAL SOLUTIONS VS. ADAPTIVE SOLUTIONS

Standard Approach and Outcome:

- Rely on familiar, technical solutions for new problems.
- Example: Mary assumed all SNTs were the same and she could rely on her CPA skills to manage them.
- Outcome: Short-term fixes that do not address deeper issues.

Counterintuitive Approach and Expected Outcome:

- Embrace adaptive solutions that involve changing behaviors and assumptions.
- Example: Mary realizes relying on her CPA skills to manage SNTs was flawed approach and *let go* of what she knew to embrace adaptive challenges ahead on path to becoming skilled administrator of SNTs.

- Expected Outcome: Sustainable, long-term adaptive solution that resolves underlying causes.

3. AVOIDING COMPLEXITIES VS. EMBRACING UNCERTAINTIES

Standard Approach and Outcome:
- Avoid dealing with complexities and uncertainties.
- Example: Mary initially avoided understanding complexities of SNTs, leading to administrative issues and mistakes.
- Outcome: Short-term relief but persistent problems.

Counterintuitive Approach and Expected Outcome:
- Accept uncertainties and embrace adaptive challenges.
- Example: Mary initially used her CPA skills to manage SNTs, realizes this approach was flawed and embraced adaptive change by attending a specialized class.
- Expected Outcome: Effective problem-solving and professional growth.

CHAPTER 4

RECOGNIZING THAT ADAPTING IS A WIN-WIN

N THE OPENING CHAPTER, WE DEFINED PROBLEMS AS the gap between what we expect and what we actually have. Then, in the second chapter, we introduced the concept of adaptive challenges, i.e., ones that can't be fixed by simply applying known technical solutions. That's because, with adaptive challenges, the problems are unknown, which is also why it's so important not just to get help but the right help. Then, in Chapter 3, we explained how adaptive change requires that you enter the gate, embracing the need to adapt *who you are* before you can close the gap.

Tackling adaptive challenges requires more than just the standard approach, more than just developing *this week's* solution. Instead, we have to genuinely rethink our approach and look through the correct lens to see the blind spots, which allows us to better see our real situation. As we mentioned in Chapter 2, solving an adaptive challenge isn't about having all the right answers or a clear plan. It's about taking steps to check our assumptions and align our actions with our values. And as described in Chapter 3, it's about seeing and challenging assumptions and deciding to enter the gate to adaptive change—a mindset shift away from focusing on changing your external reality and toward a new focus on changing *you*.

In the world of wealth management, professional fiduciary firms face these dilemmas all the time where there are gaps between what they have and what they want. They often find themselves in tough spots where they have to rely on their values to make hard decisions, even when none of the options seem great. These tough choices can make the gap between expectations and reality even bigger. However, by understanding adaptive challenges and the need to act while also reexamining our values, beliefs, and behaviors, we can develop our ability to select the right lens to see these complex problems clearly. This approach helps us navigate situations where it seems there's no good choice and no clear winner.

BETWEEN A ROCK AND A HARD PLACE

As we explained in earlier chapters, the post-GLBA era was a time when more financial firms diversified into both banking and securities business lines to engage in a broader array of financial products and services. This was arguably the beginning of what has developed into today's wealth management industry. And it is a huge industry, despite the fact that no one is quite certain what "wealth management" actually means.

Large wealth management firms often advertise a comprehensive approach for mid- to high-net-worth individuals, offering such clients a variety of services to grow their wealth, handle their taxes, and implement strategies to pass on their wealth to their heirs. These firms tout their holistic approach, comparing themselves favorably with advisors who provide only brokerage services or bank trust departments who provide only trust administration services. Yet those same, more narrowly identified "advisors," "trust departments," and even other niche players who provide just a slice of what such clients want—such as estate planners or CPAs—will themselves tout the "wealth management" services they can provide to clients, despite the smaller scope of services they offer. The bottom line is that in this day and age, many financial services firms lean into the term "wealth management" to cater to a larger customer base of not only baby boomers but also their adult children and grand-children who are themselves working to build their own wealth.

Prior to the passage of the GLBA, all those same services were indeed offered, but a customer would have likely had to do business with a number of separate firms to obtain them. The post-GLBA era saw financial institutions grab the opportunity to offer a complete package of personal financial services, and thus began a wholesale marketing of these services as com-prehensive wealth management solutions. This was seen as a win-win for many financial services firms. It allowed them to diversify their revenue streams—a win for them—and better meet the evolving personal financial services needs of their clients—a win for the clients—who could get financial plan-ning, investment advice and management, trust administration, estate settlement, and insurance solutions all under one roof and, in many cases, with just a single point of contact at a wealth management firm.

The entry of these previously siloed financial services firms into broader wealth management organizations, particularly the entry of broker-dealer and RIA firms into trust services, led to significant changes in the industry. Firms began to merge and acquire smaller specialist shops to consolidate their service offerings and provide greater convenience for their clients. This consolidation helped them stay competitive in the new era of comprehensive wealth management. It also reshaped the financial services industry.

Various organizations had to decide if or when to add wealth management to their service offerings. Many entered businesses that they did not know very much about, as we saw in Chapter 1 with George and the trust company he had to manage. Boutique firms that previously catered to a very select clientele were faced with having to decide whether to enter the wealth management industry or risk irrelevance when that same clientele wanted "comprehensive wealth management" services under one roof.

Financial services industry participants were placed, intentionally or not, in a dilemma: either they could enter wealth management and adapt to the changing landscape or remain independent and struggle for survival.

As the growth in firms offering comprehensive wealth management services continued, a few significant assumptions emerged among financial services firms.

First was the assumption that the GLBA would lead to significant changes in financial services, which it did. The financial services firms assumed this would then reshape the industry and create new opportunities for them, which also happened.

But those same firms also assumed that the regulatory framework that was supposed to be established post-GLBA would be favorable for the integration of banking, including retail and commercial banking, along with trust services, investment management, brokerage, and insurance services. They assumed that regulations that were supposed to come out under the new laws would provide the necessary framework and guidelines to successfully navigate the new landscape of comprehensive wealth management.

These assumptions influenced the decisions made by many firms as the wealth management industry grew, guiding their strategies and actions. Perhaps the biggest assumption was that financial services firms could be merged and joined and added piecemeal into a larger wealth management organization and still operate in the same manner as they had previously, when they were wholly independent.

Hindsight being 20/20, it is easy to look back and opine that what went wrong was the fault of the various regulators—bank regulators, securities and brokerage regulators, insurance regulators—who collectively failed to corral the various and oft conflicting separate regulatory frameworks, resulting in the current struggles faced by different factions within the wealth management industry. While there may be some truth to that, the fact remains that many wealth management firms have taken advantage of the opportunity to provide comprehensive financial services solutions for their clients. Within those organizations, however, we have seen over and over how professional fiduciary firms, in particular, continue to struggle to operate effectively, while also remaining true to trustee duties and responsibilities under common law. We have taken to referring to this particular dilemma as the *wealth management contradiction.*

This contradiction can be seen when a professional fiduciary firm feels pressure by the larger wealth management organization to be loyal to the wealthy individual who was their client originally, before that individual moved their assets into an irrevocable trust. The professional fiduciary firm administers that trust and must remain true to fiduciary duties and the trust beneficiaries, both current and future. The professional fiduciary firm understands that for them the *trust itself* is the client. Yet to the larger wealth management organization, the wealthy individual—the grantor of that irrevocable trust—is still the only client and still has the right to direct activities of the trust. The professional fiduciary firm understands this is wrong, but convincing the larger wealth management organization that the trust itself is "the client" becomes a battle.

What we've seen and heard from many professional fiduciary firms trying to adapt inside this wealth management contradiction is that adaptive change is stymied not out of lack of concern or effort, but rather because the professional fiduciary firm is trying to accommodate client needs for *both* the trust *and* the wealthy individual, even though they know full well that their common law duty of loyalty lies only on the side of the trust.

What they don't realize, however, is that inside their dilemma lies a win-win solution.

In the most basic terms, the goal of any adaptive solution is to identify blind spots and figure out how to adjust to whatever new environment may have emerged. In the case of the wealth management industry, savvy professional fiduciary firms know that when they encounter problems or gaps, what they are seeing, in all likelihood, is their own difficulty adapting to changes within the wealth management industry.

For example, professional fiduciary firms used to dealing directly with the interested parties of a trust, whether those individuals were the living grantors or current beneficiaries, would find it difficult to accept that a financial advisor, who was not even an employee of the professional fiduciary firm that held the trust license, actually owned the client relationship—and in some instances (probably more than professional fiduciary firms would care to admit) even managed that client relationship to the point of trying to tell the professional fiduciary firm how to administer the trust.

Adapting to a new environment is complicated. Almost by

definition. As you may recall from Chapter 2, adaptive solutions are specifically intended for problems that can't be solved with routine, technical fixes. This is also why adaptive solutions can be so hard to agree on within an organization.

With a technical fix—where the solution is already in the company's (or their consultant's) repertoire—usually there's no disagreement. But when professional fiduciary firms are asked to do something outside their existing skillsets or comfort zone, many resist. They respond to the proposed solution by listing out all the perceived risks involved, with the most significant being the risk of being sued for breach of fiduciary duty.

It can be a frustrating dynamic for everyone. One side tries to show the dangers of staying the course. The other beats the opposite drum, about all the perils the change could bring. Meanwhile, the original problem just gets worse. The gap continues to grow. How do you break this impasse?

Surprising as it may seem, the answer lies not in compromise.

In a compromise, both sides have to give something up. But here, the whole idea is to identify internal contradictions and cultivate resilience. This means optimizing the solution: getting the best of both sides. The good things about your current environment that you want to keep. The bad things you want to lose. The risks of the new environment, the things you want to avoid. And the benefits of the new environment, the things you want to gain.

An adaptive solution is, and must be arrived at as, a win-win solution.

JOANNE'S WIN-WIN

JOANNE: When I think of creating an adaptive solution, I'm reminded of my experience immigrating to the US. It was around the time I turned forty, and I'd lived and worked most of my life in Canada, where I was born and raised.

At this point in my life, I was about to be a single mom to my eight-year-old son, Ben. His father and I had recently separated, which meant I had some major life decisions to make. The idea behind moving to the States was that I could do the same kind of work but wouldn't have to travel all the time for business like for my job in Canada.

There were drawbacks, though. Or so I thought at the time. It's not so much that I myself was yearning to make this big life change. In fact, the whole thing scared me. If anything, it felt like change was being forced upon me by circumstances beyond my control. But the fact of the matter was my environment had indeed morphed into something new and different, so I had no choice but to adapt. I was suddenly a single mom. I still needed a job, needed to make money. But I also needed to build a new life for Ben.

I already had a job offer from an American bank owned by the Canadian bank I worked for, which happened to be the same one where Matt worked. We knew each other professionally and it was his boss who'd extended the job offer. As I was grappling with whether or not to shake up my and Ben's life in such a big way, I had an unexpected conversation with Matt that really changed the way I looked at my dilemma.

Up to this point, I had been worrying about all the things I would have to give up by moving to the US. As I told Matt during a phone call where I was debating the wisdom of accepting the job, I loved my country, Canada, and was sad to think about losing it. I'll always remember his response: "Why not move to the US? Do you think you'd be losing your country? You're not losing anything, in fact, you're gaining another country. You'll have two great places you can call home!"

He was 100 percent right. And for me this conversation seemed to sow the seed of how we both came to think about adaptive change in general.

I know that Matt's words helped shift my thinking away from all the "don't change" reasons to make such a major life adjustment to more of the "why change" reasons, giving me hope that I could change, take that new job in the US, and still hang onto the things I liked about my known, comfortable environment—my life in Canada.

So, I accepted the job offer and moved to the US. But I also recognized that for me, I knew if I was going to do this, I was going to be all in. I didn't want to settle for a temporary work visa and merely count down the twenty-four months until it expired and I had to return to Canada. I became determined to take the path to US citizenship and embrace the opportunity of a brand new life in the US for both myself and Ben. One that would truly give us two countries we could call home if we chose to become dual citizens.

That's exactly what we did. And it was a true win-win solution. In my new job, I got to expand my knowledge and skills, gaining a newfound joy in my career. And I gained the benefit of not having to travel for work so I could spend more quality time with my son. During the summers, Ben got to vacation with his dad in Canada, and I also got to spend some of my vacation time there, visiting family and friends and staying connected to my Canadian roots.

Five years later, however, I faced another dilemma. Ben was about to enter high school and was too old for before- and after-school daycare. Although I really loved my job at the bank as a senior level compliance officer, and was grateful for all they'd done for me, I didn't love the idea of my son being a teenage latchkey kid. I wanted to be there every day when he got home from school.

By this point, I had obtained my and Ben's green cards—something my bank had sponsored. Also by this point, as it happened, Matt had left the bank and started his own company, Nth Degree. When he heard about my new dilemma, whether to keep the job I loved (and needed for the paycheck it provided) or be home more for Ben, he made an unexpected suggestion: "Why not quit the bank and join my company?" Immediately, my brain responded with all the reasons I couldn't possibly do that. I remember telling Matt, "I can't, that job is my security! How am I going to afford to live?"

But eventually, like with my earlier dilemma about losing my home country and taking a new job in the US, Matt's words resonated and gave me hope that just maybe I could still keep all the good things I liked about my existing environment—living in the US, seeing Ben thrive—while obtaining the new benefits of having flexible working hours where I could be home when Ben got out of school.

I recognized this had happened once before for me when I faced a dilemma, when my thinking had shifted away from all the "don't change" reasons I told myself in order to convince me not to change, to the "why change" reasons. It was then I realized this could be another win-win situation, for both me and Ben. I didn't have to be scared of the change, scared to relinquish a job I loved, even though it was keeping me from doing what I knew was really important for me—to be with Ben more as he entered his high-school years.

Though I was afraid of what the future might bring and afraid my earnings might drop, I realized I didn't have to compromise. I figured, worst case scenario, since I already had my green card, if working for Matt's company didn't pan out, I could always just get another job. And in the meantime, for Ben's high-school years, I would have the job flexibility I wanted. With that win-win solution, I realized I would have the best of all worlds.

MERMAIDS, ALLIGATORS, POTS OF GOLD, AND CRUTCHES

When we work with professional fiduciary firms, we almost always encounter some people on the team who have perfectly good reasons to dig in their heels and do not want to change anything. Then, there's often another group of a few people who take the opposite side and seem to want to change everything.

As for the former, it's not that they're just being stubborn or uncooperative. But they're hesitant, and, like Joanne herself experienced when faced with major dilemmas, don't want to lose all the good things they like about their current environment.

It's very important to see their side of things—the "don't change" side.

Why don't they want to change?

On the one hand, from our perspective as consultants, deep down we know that every improvement requires change, but not every change is an improvement! So we make every effort to hear from them directly about all the good things they have and believe should be retained. Over the years we have learned that this information is crucially important and valuable.

EVERY IMPROVEMENT REQUIRES
CHANGE, BUT NOT EVERY
CHANGE IS AN IMPROVEMENT!

Unlike providing consulting services that require just a technical solution, such as an updated policy manual or refreshed risk assessment, when facing an adaptive challenge—where the problem is not known and the solution not clearly understood—it's not just about *what* has to change, but *why change.*

The more we worked with professional fiduciary firms, the more we noticed the same recurring dynamic among their teams, and this is how we came to understand the importance of the win-win concept.

We even borrowed nomenclature around it from Matt's mentor Dr. Eli Goldratt's last publication, *Isn't It Obvious*, published in July 2010, which deals with overcoming resistance to change within organizations and puts forth the following framework: In your current environment, there are the good things that you like and want to keep, called *mermaids*. There are also the bad things that are dangerous that you will need to eliminate, called *alligators*. Be careful. They have sharp teeth![15]

As for the new environment that lies on the other side of a proposed change, there are, of course, all the benefits that await, the things you want to gain, called *pots of gold*. But there are also difficult challenges ahead, the places where you could make mistakes and get seriously hurt, called *crutches*.

People on the "don't change" side are generally the ones who can see the *mermaids*—the benefits of staying the same—in the current environment and also the *crutches*—the dangers of changing—in the new environment. Or at least that's what they're focused on.

People on the "change" side are generally the ones who can see the *alligators*—the dangers of staying the same—in the current environment and the *pots of gold*—the benefits of making the change—in the future environment, but who are quick to dismiss the value of the mermaids and crutches.

As we stated earlier, the path forward must be found *not* in compromise, where both sides feel they've had to give up something. Rather, it's through the process of overcoming resistance to change—by identifying the mermaids, alligators, pots of gold, and crutches—that everyone will be able to see the value in adopting an adaptive solution, leading to a win-win solution where both sides feel they've won.

And the way to get there is to dig into the why—*why* change?—not just the what.

Joanne had gone through this same process during two major life changes. When struggling with whether to move to the US, Matt's words got her considering the "why change" reasons to move. Joanne had spent a little time living and working in the States before, and had loved it. This opportunity for a permanent move was a pot of gold—she could live in the US and take the path to citizenship, gaining a new country. And not having to travel for business meant she was able to get rid of a huge alligator. Win-win! She was also able to retain what she liked, the mermaid of keeping strong ties with her home country of Canada.

The same held true five years later, when Matt's words got her thinking about the "why change" reasons she should quit the bank. Joanne could take a job with Nth Degree and have the pot of gold that came with flexible hours while still earning a living. And she would be getting rid of another alligator with Ben not having to be a latchkey teenager. Again, win-win! She was also able to retain what she loved about her job, the mermaid of being able to continue to expand her knowledge and skills while earning a living.

A CAUTIONARY TALE ABOUT NEGLECTING THE WHY

Joanne recalls a US client she helped many moons ago, well before her permanent move to the States. At the time, she was working for a Canadian software company and one of their biggest clients was a major New York bank, a huge organization doing full financial services—investments, brokerage, trust, a whole gamut of post-GLBA era wealth management service—but at a time that was way ahead of the curve because this pre-dated the GLBA by about ten years. (Yes, Congress sometimes enacts laws well after an industry has already changed—just ask where the laws are for the crypto industry, launched in January 2009 when Bitcoin was created.)

This particular US bank wanted to buy software from the Canadian company where Joanne worked. They were going to use it to provide front-, middle-, and back-office solutions, but their primary focus was on their investment management and trading activities. They actually bought the source code from the Canadian company so they could make programming changes themselves. They had their own big international IT team, which worked with the Canadian company's programming team for a full year to implement the new software.

Joanne was brought in to train the NY bank employees on how to use the software to produce the correct results. She ended up spending almost a year living and working in midtown Manhattan—and loving it. In fact, it was a big part of why she decided later to immigrate to the US. But as much as she enjoyed her time in the Big Apple, she couldn't say the same about the time she spent with the client!

In fact, she remembers the first time she tried to train the traders—just a few months before the conversion date when the new software would go live—and how badly it went. Imagine a room full of NYC traders, all men, all skilled at their craft, all used to old-school trading methods of working the phones and filling out paper trading tickets that their assistants would then enter into their old system. This was the late eighties, right around the time Oliver Stone's *Wall Street* came out. And it was late in the day, after the New York Stock Exchange closed. The traders clearly didn't want to be there—they wanted to be on their way home. So they were kind of belligerent about having to stay at work.

They also made it clear they *really* didn't want to use the new system. They didn't want to use *any* system. They liked the old manual way of trading. They wanted to keep working the phones and filling out written trade tickets while their assistants learned the new system to do the mundane data entry. Yet here was Joanne, trying to teach these guys, two dozen of them, in a windowless training room, at the end of a long trading day, with each trader sitting in front of a terminal that connected via dial-up modem to the mainframe computer-based trading software. She couldn't even get them past the initial step of signing on with their username and password, particularly after a trader asked if the terminal was a computer and Joanne said, no, they are just dummy terminals that connect to the mainframe computer. She realized as soon as the words were out of her mouth that the entire room had turned against her. They didn't realize "dummy terminal" was a computer term; they thought Joanne was implying they were too dumb to use the real computer and only got fake equipment, while other people would get to use real computers.

That whole first session was a disaster. Not only did none of the traders want to change, but they were completely uncooperative. Joanne couldn't get any of those guys past both the dial-up and sign-on screens. Most of them just slapped willy-nilly at the keyboard, and two of the traders at the back of the room secretly unplugged their terminals then complained their equipment didn't work.

Joanne and her colleagues at the software company had encountered this kind of resistance on the part of traders to using a keyboard instead of hand-written trading tickets, but never to this extent. Their Canadian clients tended to be more mild-mannered, at least on the surface. This was a whole new level of resistance she had not had to deal with before. In looking back now, Joanne realizes she was just a kid, and a naïve Canadian one at that, who was overwhelmed by this brash group of New York traders. But she knew that the only reason she had been given this opportunity to live and work in Manhattan, a place she'd always longed to visit, was that her boss believed she could handle the job. Joanne was not a quitter and tried to come up with a solution to get the traders trained—and fast, since that would be integral to the overall success of the new system. Joanne needed a solution that was a win for her, with traders trained and her boss pleased, as well as a win for the traders. They would learn not only how to use a keyboard; they would also discover how impressive the trading software was and love it once they realized its capabilities. In other words, Joanne instinctively knew she had to let them see the *why change* side of the equation, not just the *what* had to change.

Long story short: eventually the bank converted to the new system, but partly because of the egos involved, and the need to ensure there was a win-win solution, Joanne had been forced to develop a custom training solution for virtually every trader. It was nuts. And by custom training solution, we mean literally a one-on-one training effort for every trader, often after hours, and always with no other traders present to prevent egos from taking over. Joanne had to first listen to each trader to learn and understand the old phone- and paper-based trading system they personally used, so she could then walk each of them step by step through the process of how to do what they did before, but even better and faster by using the new software. She also had to demonstrate for them all the new capabilities the system offered for trading the complex derivatives just then coming into vogue.

As a side note, some years later, long after Joanne was out of the picture, she was captivated by a series of newspaper articles about that same bank's very public failures, which eventually resulted in their going out of business—due to investment and trading issues that had nothing to do with the failure of the software, but which the advanced software system may very well have accelerated.

Joanne wondered then if the software solution itself had been a compromise solution implemented by the bank to close a gap.

What was the real story? Joanne knew that at the time her company had been brought in, the NY bank had just gone through a change in leadership. While working at their Manhattan offices, she'd heard around the proverbial water cooler that the new president was essentially forcing a technical solution with the new software in an attempt to enhance their investment and trading prowess, already well regarded on Wall Street, in order to greatly increase profitability—and his own business reputation. While the investment and trading employees knew *what* was changing, they had no real idea *why* they were changing. They saw only the things they liked, the mermaids, about their prior system (which was going away without them having been able to participate in that decision) and didn't see the alligator of falling profits that the president was trying to get rid of. No wonder those traders were resistant.

The bank's own programmers were also upset because their proprietary system, which had served them well for many years, was being thrown out and replaced with this new software from a small company in Canada that no one else on the Street was using. Only a select few individuals at the bank's international office understood the pots of gold offered with the new technology, software that would handle with ease that international office's complex multi-currency derivatives investments and trading activities. And it seems no one saw the crutches waiting on the other side of the change—the risks of the change that may have inadvertently accelerated the bank's eventual downfall.

As with most such technical solutions, there was almost certainly a genuine need for the new software. The investment and trading environment had indeed changed and became a riskier place in the eighties and nineties for financial institutions. As with many Wall Street firms at the time, it's possible the NY bank president had become concerned about managing its overall investment risk. The growth in financial derivatives was widely seen by the industry as a way to "hedge," or reduce, those risks.

In recalling those wild Wall Street years, Joanne realizes it's likely the president did not err in embracing a technical solution to help the bank enhance its investment and trading, while increasing profits. The *what* was clear and, back then, improving the bottom line was a common enough *why* for an organization to implement a technical solution. For the employees impacted by the change, however—those traders who Joanne discovered were completely resistant to using the new software—there was no logic to the change. And Joanne remembers them complaining they didn't know *why* they had to change their trading system.

If those same traders, years later, didn't see the benefits of the *why change*—the pot of gold that the new derivatives trading capabilities could bring to managing investment risk—Joanne now wonders if that NY bank could have avoided their public failures and ultimate downfall, the crutches of the change, if the *why change* had been fully understood and embraced.

Instead, back then it was all about the *what*. As in: this is *what* you are going to do whether you like it or not. And there's the door if you don't fall into line.

WHERE DOES THE TRUSTED CONSULTANT FIT IN?

In that story, perhaps if Joanne and her bosses at the software company had the knowledge necessary to implement an adaptive solution, they might have been able to do more to connect with the NY bank president and the traders as they introduced the new system capabilities. They could have helped them see not only the benefits of the *why change* and worked with them to retain the mermaids of their old processes, those things that were well-known and just worked well, while the alligators would vanish once the new system was operational. Then, more attention could have been paid to avoiding the risks of the system's advanced capabilities, those crutches that may have been accelerated their downfall.

Joanne's bosses at her software company could have tried to address the gap between the naysayers and the bank president, so that the two sides might have been able to come together in a meaningful way—all toward preventing mistakes and avoiding risks.

Had this been done correctly, it's tempting to imagine that the new software and all of the new processes developed around it, properly used, may even have been able to save the bank. But the industry didn't understand adaptive change back then and Joanne's company certainly didn't have the language, or even the confidence, to communicate it to a large NY bank driven by its brash investment management and trading activities.

If Joanne and her bosses at the software company had taken an adaptive approach from the start, they would have also had to lead the bank president toward a new way of thinking. Which begs the question: how would they have been able to accomplish that? After all, he was the one paying them to implement his preferred technical solution. Doesn't the buck stop with him?

Yes and no.

While it's true that the leadership in your own wealth management organization holds formal authority around such decisions, there is more to it, as we'll see in the following chapter.

RECOGNIZING THAT ADAPTING IS A WIN-WIN

1. TECHNICAL FIXES VS. ADAPTIVE SOLUTIONS

Standard Approach and Outcome:

- Use technical fixes to solve problems with existing knowledge and processes.
- Example: George raised fees and hired a new salesperson to fix the trust company's issues without addressing the underlying adaptive challenges.
- Outcome: Quick fixes to get the problem resolved. Alleviate discomfort of problem.

Counterintuitive Approach and Expected Outcome:

- Embrace adaptive solutions that involve reevaluating values and mindsets.
- Example: Recognize need to adapt to the wealth management environment and align values accordingly.
- Expected Outcome: Sustainable, long-term adaptive solutions that resolve root causes.

2. COMPROMISE VS. WIN-WIN SOLUTIONS

Standard Approach and Outcome:

- Seek compromises where both sides give something up.
- Example: Professional fiduciary firms compromising between trust administration and financial advisor demands without finding a true resolution.
- Outcome: Partial technical solutions that may not fully address the problem.

Counterintuitive Approach and Expected Outcome:

- Aim for win-win adaptive solutions to optimize benefits for both sides.
- Example: Joanne's decisions to move to the US and join Nth Degree, achieves personal and professional satisfaction without compromising her values.
- Expected Outcome: Effective, mutually beneficial outcomes that address all aspects of the problem.

3. RESISTANCE TO CHANGE VS. EMBRACING ADAPTIVE CHANGE

Standard Approach and Outcome:

- Resist change to preserve familiar and comfortable routines.
- Example: Traders at the New York bank resisting new trading software due to attachment to old manual methods.
- Outcome: Safety in approach. Known solutions. Risk averse.

Counterintuitive Approach and Expected Outcome:

- Embrace adaptive change by understanding and addressing the "why" behind the change.
- Example: Joanne shifts mindset to see benefits of moving to US and later changes jobs to better support her son.
- Expected Outcome: Successful adaptive change and improvement in performance and satisfaction.

CHAPTER 5

LEVERAGING INFORMAL AUTHORITY

S IT TURNS OUT, *FORMAL* AUTHORITY—LIKE THE KIND held by the Manhattan bank president in the story from Chapter 4—is insufficient on its own to bring about successful, sustainable adaptive change.

How can that be? The answer is there are simply too many constraints on the person holding that formal authority, too many specific expectations placed upon them. At least in the context of trying to bring about adaptive change.

Formal authority is fine for a technical solution: the boss decides to hire more trust officers, move to a new location, get a new trust accounting system, outsource investment management, or whatever the case may be where a technical change is what's needed. As far as the corporate organization is concerned, the boss can make the decision for a technical solution and that's that—the staff will get on board to implement the change.

When it comes to adaptive change, however, where a professional fiduciary firm (and those who work in it) has to change its values, beliefs, and behaviors, where it must enter the gate into a new perspective and change (or even decide to *not* change) to achieve a desired win-win solution, the person in the organization with the formal authority will not be able to effectively mandate these things at all.

That's why relying on formal authorities and organizational hierarchies is insufficient when adaptive change is needed. Instead, professional fiduciary firms, and those who work there, need to harness the power of *informal* authority, to both initiate and then effectively navigate the necessary adaptive change initiatives to achieve desired outcomes.

But what exactly *is* informal authority? And how can it possibly be that you—and other internal stakeholders (plus some external ones, as we'll see shortly)—have the power to effect adaptive change in a way that even your CEO likely doesn't?

In order to answer these questions, we need to take a step back. Remember in Chapter 2 how we talked about the importance of procuring the right help? What we meant is that the "right help," whether that comes from outside the organization or even from within, understands the difference between technical and adaptive challenges.

Traditionally, however, professional fiduciary firms sought help from external experts, including us, strictly for technical solutions.

Here's what it often looks like. A prospective client will reach out with a problem, or set of problems, they believe we can fix. And in most cases, so do we. We know we have the expertise to address their technical challenges, such as completing documentation for de novo trust license applications, writing policies and procedures, conducting fiduciary risk assessments, or even performing audits or compliance testing. We can confidently assure the prospective client we can help them with a solution to resolve their problem. Moreover, we can often complete such work with little to no disruption to them, and minimal effort or involvement on their part.

That's because we know in advance all they need is a technical solution.

Situations like this are pretty easy to resolve. The client has a known problem and realistic expectations. We provide a clear solution. The client can see the problem, and we can help define it, provide the solution if it lies within our capabilities, or recommend other experts to implement a technical solution.

This is the kind of work consultants to professional fiduciary firms have traditionally provided. And while somewhat mechanical in nature, the work is nonetheless valuable for the client.

In recent years, however, we've started to notice a change. What we're seeing more and more is that clients will approach us with problems they can't clearly see, problems that are not purely technical and require more than just technical expertise. Instead of problems that need only a technical solution, these are situations that demand a collaborative effort between the consultant and the client. Unlike with a technical solution, which asks for minimal effort or involvement from the client, for problems that require more than just technical expertise the responsibility for defining and addressing the problem and closing the gap is, and must be, shared. The client cannot simply transfer all responsibility to the consultant. Rather, the two sides must collaborate to uncover hidden assumptions and beliefs, challenge conventional thinking, and develop adaptive solutions to address the core issues—the invisible threats hidden in the fog.

And it's here, in tackling these adaptive challenges, that we first see the need for informal authority.

We see it, initially, in the figure of the consultant, who must be able to guide the client and help them effectively navigate through the adaptive challenge. The consultant does that by leveraging their own informal authority. This authority is derived not from an organizational, hierarchical position but rather from their expertise and credibility, as well as their crucial ability to build rapport with the people who work for the firm. The consultant draws upon this informal authority to exert certain influence but, unlike with a technical challenge, does not simply take over and provide a ready-made solution. Instead, the consultant's informal authority helps facilitate the shared responsibility to empower the client to take ownership of the problem-solving process. This is the point where the client enters the gate and actively participates in identifying and implementing the necessary changes.

In this process, the consultant uses their informal authority to take on a more strategic role with the client. Instead of just offering technical solutions, they help the client explore the hidden assumptions and beliefs. The consultant's role here is to ask the right questions, encouraging the client to embrace the discomfort of entering the gate to adaptive change, all toward creating an environment that fosters learning, growth, and innovation. Ultimately, the consultant's informal authority helps the client develop a deeper understanding of their own internal dynamics and gain the confidence and skills needed to navigate future adaptive challenges.

This is the power and potential of informal authority. And in the same way that the consultant uses it to influence and effect change outside of the client's formal hierarchies, so too must professional fiduciary firms, and those who work for them, harness this power within their organizations.

They must do so because, as we stated at the top of this chapter, formal authority is largely ineffective when it comes to situations that call for adaptive change. The person or people at the top holding formal authority in professional fiduciary organizations are hamstrung by all sorts of institutional factors.

The important point here is that even without formal power or explicit authorization—sometimes precisely because of the fact that formal authority is absent—it is possible to embrace adaptive change and implement sustainable solutions to vanquish the Invisible Threat and close the gap.

It is not an exaggeration to say that informal authority is the spark that will ignite the adaptive revolution. Through this chapter, we look at how to develop and leverage informal authority within your professional fiduciary firm toward this ambitious long-term goal of achieving adaptive change.

INFORMAL AUTHORITY IS THE SPARK THAT IGNITES THE ADAPTIVE REVOLUTION.

These same principles can also apply to any group of people who find themselves having to work through problems by seeing and challenging their values, beliefs, and behaviors. And to any situation where informal authority is just the spark needed to ignite adaptive change.

For example, it was through her own family upbringing that Joanne came to understand the power of informal authority.

A NEW ROLE FOR JOANNE

JOANNE: It was clear to me from an early age that my mom held the formal authority within our large family. But starting when I was only five years old, strange as this may sound given I was still just a little girl, I developed informal authority in our household.

This all happened in a way I couldn't fully understand at the time. But I definitely felt it. I was not sure if I even liked it. But it did make me proud to serve this crucial role inside our family unit.

What's remarkable is how this dynamic—established back when we were kids still growing up more than half a century ago—has endured through the decades. It continues to serve us, me and my six siblings, to this day, even with our parents gone, though it now ebbs and flows with changing circumstances and my awareness that I have to maintain their trust to keep that informal authority.

How did I find myself in this unlikely role? I'm not the oldest sibling. In fact, I was the youngest of three daughters. But then my parents went and had three more kids: two more girls—twins!—followed by my very first brother. This shuffled the hierarchy and catapulted me up to third oldest sibling out of six. Or if you count the twins as a unit, third out of five, right in the middle. And that's how I was seen, as the middle child. But my informal authority in our household wasn't about age so much as the unusual circumstances behind its emergence. This all began when I was about to go to kindergarten. I had just turned five that August and my two older sisters had already gone to kindergarten before me (one was now enrolled in first grade, the other in third). I was so excited to finally get to go to school like them.

I had also recently acquired those two younger siblings—the twins! I was three and a half years old when they were born, and it was as if suddenly I went from being the cherished baby of the family to an afterthought. Not that my parents didn't care about me anymore. But with not just one but an unexpected two new babies, obviously their hands were full. Oh, and on top of that, my mom was pregnant again, and less than two months away from giving birth to my first brother. When the day came for my mom to register me for kindergarten at the local school, she had quite the baby bump.

We arrived at the school—me, Mom, and the twins in their stroller—and had to wait in a long line to register. I didn't mind, I was just so excited to be there. When we reached the front of the line, the woman in charge of registration looked up at my visibly pregnant mom. Then, she looked at the twins, barely a year old, in their stroller. And at me. Then, she looked at my mom and told her the school was very crowded that year. If my mom wanted, she could keep me home from kindergarten to help out around the house. She wouldn't be breaking any truancy laws. She explained that because of the large number of students—it was still the Baby Boom years—the school was allowing kids who didn't attend kindergarten that year to go directly into first grade the following year.

I remember my mom trying to absorb the words, looking down at me then back at the woman and saying okay. And with that, my longed-for kindergarten year vanished.

I was heartbroken when my mom turned away and headed back home. As we walked along, my mom told me I was going to be her little helper that year. She wasn't kidding. Especially after my brother was born the next month and our home routine changed in a big way. With both my new brother and the twins at home, now I was always bathing one or another of them, getting them dressed, feeding them, taking them for walks, and keeping them entertained so they wouldn't cry.

I actually loved it. Loved the responsibility. Loved helping my mom. I felt such a strong connection with her.

Every afternoon, once she'd put my brother and the twins down for their nap, my mother promised that if I was good, washed the lunch dishes, and tidied up the kitchen so my mom could also rest, after naptime she would go to the library across the street and get a book just for me. Then, in what I think of now as a magic moment in time, while she waited for the kettle to boil water for our afternoon tea, my mom would sit beside me at our kitchen table and read that day's book to me. It reminded me of what life had been like before the twins were born and everything got so busy—when I was still the baby of the family. Our mom used to read to me and my older sisters in the evenings as we cuddled up next to her on the couch, with my dad relaxing in his easy chair. Those afternoons when my mom read to me gave me some of those feelings back. It was extra magical because it was just me and my mom as I got to listen to her read me a new story every weekday afternoon during what should have been my kindergarten school year.

I suspect that was the seed that led to my lifelong love of books and reading. More important to me at the time, however, was by helping her with the babies and the household chores, as a reward I got to spend a lot of quality time with my mom—which I cherished, especially after having felt jealous of the twins at first.

Through my close connection with my mom during this period, I also gained a new understanding of her busy life and the burdens she shouldered. With a husband and six kids (three in cloth diapers), between cooking for everyone, cleaning clothes, keep the house tidy, and doing all the household shopping...well, it was a lot. Inevitably, my mom's temper would flare up. Not something anyone in our family wanted. By spending so much time with her that year, I discovered there were things I could do to make her more relaxed and prevent her temper from getting the better of her. I started to share those things with my siblings, even my older sisters, to try to get them to behave better and help out around the house more.

This was how I started to gain informal authority—and learn how to use it.

I would try to see and identify conflicts, invisible threats that could cause my mom to lose her temper, before they arose. For example, my older sisters and I were supposed to clean up the kitchen right away after dinner, but if they were goofing around and doing a poor job—which I knew would upset my mom and ruin any chance of a peaceful family evening—I wouldn't boss them around directly. I knew that wouldn't work because they were older and wouldn't listen to me. Instead, I would encourage their cooperation by asking, "Should we get this done so mom doesn't get mad?" then jump right in by clearing the table.

I even did this a bit with my dad. Obviously, I had no formal authority in that parental relationship. He was my dad. An adult. I was a kid and he was hyper aware of anyone (except my mom!) trying to boss him around. Over time I noticed it shifted the dynamic somehow. He started to defer to me, probably realizing my encouragement for different behaviors would, after all, result in a more enjoyable home life for him as well. Just like with my older sisters, though, if he sensed I was being bossy, he'd pay no attention to me.

With time, I learned to use informal influence more and more effectively. And slowly, I saw how my informal influence was seeping into both his and my older sisters' thinking and behavior. They were adapting. For example, whereas the after-dinner cleanup routine used to be a trigger point with a lot of yelling, somehow it became a standard routine where everyone just realized, *Yeah we should just do this to get it over with and Mom won't get mad.*

It was almost like I had tapped into a secret power. But what made it so effective was not its force but rather its subtlety. The more I used it over the years, the more I learned how to employ it wisely. I even used it with my mom occasionally, though she would look right at me and say I was trying to manipulate her. Which I was. Then she'd laugh and I knew all was good. But I used it most with my sisters and brother. Nowadays, if something's going in a strange direction with me and my siblings, like when we're planning for a family reunion, I am able to step in—in a gentle, informal way—and help guide the direction so the whole thing doesn't fall apart. But what's great is that I rarely have to. As siblings, even though our mom and dad have passed, the adaptive culture we embraced to succeed as a family unit during those years when we were young—and there were so many of us, including my baby brother who arrived on the scene when I was eight—has remained with us over the years.

For informal authority to be effective, the key is to guide rather than boss. Which is logical because if you lack formal authority, you cannot boss others; no one will pay attention or, worse, they'll turn against you. Informal authority only works— in any organization, whether in a family, a business, or any other type of organizational unit—when there's trust.

That doesn't happen overnight.

DEVELOPING TRUST

The reason this worked for Joanne and her family is that over time they came to trust her because year in and year out, she consistently used her informal authority to solve problems and make things better for the family. Joanne had learned at her mother's side that nothing made her mom madder than when the kids were fighting or arguing with one another. And anything could set off a sibling battle.

Joanne will be the first to admit she was not perfect and participated in her share of sibling mayhem. But early on, she recognized the pattern: their petty fights caused serious reactions up the formal chain of command to the top, and once there it would be too late; Mom would be mad and things would be miserable for everyone. So Joanne learned what triggered fights and arguments and tried to use her informal influence to prevent those triggers. Only seven cookies left in the jar and nine people who wanted one? A ten-inch round cake that had to be cut into nine perfectly even pieces? Not enough board game pieces for everyone to play? Whenever situations arose where it looked like there might be an unfair result, the family learned to turn to Joanne, who would encourage solutions where it seemed everyone came out the winner. They turned to her because of her track record. She put the family unit first—not herself, nor any particular sibling (even those trying to hustle her for a favor) but always the family unit. Joanne walked the walk consistently, over and over again.

Consistency is key. Consistency of results but also consistency of values. One essential component of trust building in this context is developing a common set of values. People must know and feel confident you are there for them and have their back—and that this is all rooted in your shared values. In Joanne's case, she always made a point of treating her siblings fairly and equally and because of that, they trusted her, even when she annoyed the heck out of them.

Trust is a word with profound meaning in the professional fiduciary industry. If you are in the business, you too will want to build your ability to use informal influence by nurturing trust. It's not instantaneous. And once earned, it has to be maintained. Even separate from developing the skillset of influencing people and outcomes through informal authority, there's the matter of understanding the mechanisms within your organization for exercising that informal authority. How can you strategize and strengthen your ability to influence across the company?

Part of it is developing rapport with the right people. Those individuals who are the existing influencers, the informal leaders. True leadership goes beyond titles and positions. It's about influence, inspiration, and the ability to motivate others toward a common goal, regardless of formal authority. Informal leaders may not get paid the big bucks of CEOs, but they have the same passion, vision, and knack for thriving in chaos. Ultimately, it is the informal leadership who will ensure the organization can influence adaptive changes to get the job done.

As we noted earlier, the actual boss, the person holding the formal authority, does not always have the power to get things done, at least in terms of adaptive change. If the boss were able to do what was needed for every situation, they would have done so a long time ago. But the fact is that because of institutional constraints, they can usually only authorize technical solutions. And since it's an adaptive change you're after when a technical solution won't fix the problem, that's simply not enough.

Thankfully, there's a great deal of power to be leveraged in those informal networks.

LEVERAGING INFORMAL
AUTHORITY IS HOW YOU GET
THINGS DONE THAT YOU ARE NOT
EXPLICITLY AUTHORIZED TO DO.

When we talk about this unexpected power found in informal networks, we're talking about real, concrete power to effect change. In fact, this ability to make things happen represents the second essential component of trust building. The first, described earlier in this chapter, was developing a common set of values. Building trust toward leveraging one's informal authority is only possible when you have an ability to execute and get the job done—not *in spite of* your lack of formal authorization but rather *because of it*.

Master these two trust-building components—developing a common set of values and being able to make things happen—and you will be well positioned to stimulate adaptive change in your professional fiduciary firm. Without it maybe you and others in your organization had developed coping mechanisms to suffer through your dilemmas, but that can't go on forever. In an adaptive environment, the way forward is to master these two trust building components with the informal authorities within your organization. Together lies the way forward.

You'll also want to keep building the adaptive muscle within your organization. How do you do that? By using the mermaids/alligators/pots of gold/crutches framework from the previous chapter. Ask what you want to gain from your future environment (pots of gold) and what you want to keep from your current environment (mermaids).

Mapping this out together within your informal network will bring your firm closer to identifying its common goal. Then, what you'll likely find is that, by exercising this adaptive muscle, things will start to happen. And not just in a single area or for a single problem. Once your brain—or maybe the collective brain of your informal network—gets into this new adaptive environment where you are no longer at an impasse and instead are on the path toward the common goal, it's like having the skies clear and the fog dissipate. This is the incredible power that can be found in informal networks and relationships that exist outside your firm's formal leadership hierarchy.

But why is it necessary to leverage informal authority in this way? Why is the formal authority inside a professional fiduciary firm limited in its ability to effect adaptive change? Let's return to Jeff, from Chapter 2, to explore the answers.

THE LIMITS OF FORMAL AUTHORITY

After accepting the right help, removing the Board Chair, and rehiring his old CFO, Jeff and his business partners still needed to raise capital to establish a South Dakota licensed trust company. But as co-leader of his group, along with his two business partners, Jeff's formal authority came with certain blind spots that got in his way as he attempted to execute his plan of eventually running a trust company.

As it turned out, it was only through the informal authority of that same trusted outside consultant from Chapter 2 that Jeff was able to see alternative solutions and, ultimately, achieve adaptive change. How so? By casually inviting Jeff to participate in a workshop series, the consultant strategically employed his informal influence to help Jeff shed his blind spots and explore new ideas and perspectives.

This is how it went down. Not long after the Board Chair exited, Jeff had reached out anew to the outside consultant for help kicking the tires on his revised business plan and ensuring that their application for the trust license would be approved.

By this point, Jeff's leadership group had been hit with a big blow when one business partner had to drop out of the plan. Apparently, a major change had cropped up in this fellow's personal family circumstances, leaving him with no choice but to break the news to Jeff and the other partner that he would no longer be able to commit the necessary capital nor, even more importantly, the time necessary to ensure the future trust company's success. Despite the blow, Jeff and his remaining partner were determined to soldier on and had developed a revised strategic plan that would pass muster with the state's licensing office.

The consultant had been involved with putting together this revised business plan, but after reviewing the final plan he was less sure of its long-term success, even though Jeff and his remaining business partner were keen to move forward. Deep down the consultant knew there was something off about it. Yes, they would probably get their trust license. But was the plan sufficient for actually running the trust company and meeting all the ongoing requirements that went along with it once the license was obtained?

The consultant wasn't so sure, but his job with Jeff was over. He had done what was asked of him, namely provide a technical solution by reviewing the revised business plan. The plan itself was sound and he advised Jeff that it would likely achieve the specific objective of getting a trust license. But the consultant also sensed that a license could cause more harm than good. He didn't know what to do about his concerns, however. He couldn't really open that door again. Or could he?

Then an opportunity arose where the consultant saw a way to exert informal influence. What happened was a former colleague of his was running a new workshop series using the Goldratt Change Matrix (the mermaids/alligators/pots of gold/ crutches framework) targeted not to business organizations but to ordinary people facing life/work challenges and dilemmas. His colleague had reached out to the consultant to see if he wanted to help facilitate these new sessions, as he had in the past with some previous workshops.

This gave the consultant an idea. Instead of just facilitating the workshops, since this new series was broadly targeted to the public and still had available participant spots open, what if he asked Jeff and his business partner if they wanted to participate? Introducing Jeff and his partner to the workshop, as participants, would provide a forum for the consultant's unease about the trust license to emerge naturally without him having to *tell* Jeff and his partner what to do, or boss them around, or in any way disrespect their formal authority.

Thankfully, the former colleague who was running the series loved the idea. So did Jeff, who, it turns out, had been starting to question their business plan himself. He knew the business idea was solid, but was that enough? Especially in light of the recent loss of his other business partner, Jeff wasn't so sure they could actually run a trust company. While his remaining business partner was unable to participate, Jeff took the consultant up on his invitation. He signed up for the series and was excited to learn about the Goldratt Change Matrix, hoping it would help him see the business challenges in a new way.

Jeff also hoped bringing his own challenging business situation to the workshop would help point him in the direction of a win-win solution. And ultimately, that is exactly what happened. Through the experience of participating in the workshop and experiencing the power of the Goldratt Change Matrix by identifying the mermaids, alligators, pots of gold, and crutches in his plan, Jeff experienced a true "ah-ha" moment.

He realized he'd been so focused on the changes he had to make, and so excited about the pots of gold that awaited his business on the other side, that he couldn't see all the crutches that came with transitioning to become a trust company—especially after the loss of one of his two business partners. He was also hearing from some of his new employees, who had previously worked for professional fiduciary firms, about their experiences with fiduciary risk and how challenging that business could be for de novo trust companies.

Jeff also saw how the alligators in his situation had become very few and far between ever since he'd fired the Board Chair and his associated consultancy group. Moreover, through the Goldratt workshop experience, he realized, for perhaps the first time, just how many mermaids or good things he already had in his current environment. His new business was already up and running, he and his business partner were bringing in new clients every day, and word of mouth meant their business was likely to continue on a path of exponential growth.

And this was all happening, Jeff realized, without them having to even obtain a trust license yet. How could that be? After all, the whole idea behind their business plan was that they needed to have their own trust company. This would protect them against losing the business to an outside trust organization whenever their clients got to the stage of life when they needed those professional fiduciary services. So a new question began to gnaw at Jeff: instead of following through with this big change to become a trust company, what if Jeff and his remaining business partner decided to *not* change? What would that cost/benefit analysis look like? Was it a viable approach? Could they continue to grow their current business and increase revenue?

Gradually, the solution became clear. What Jeff's business model really needed was the ability to provide clients with professional fiduciary services, but without their own business bearing all the costs and fiduciary risks associated with having a trust license—and, equally important, without losing those same clients to an outside wealth management firm. Was this even a possibility? Could they provide such services without being a trust company? *Why not?* Jeff wondered. *In fact, that's exactly what we do now through our outsourced arrangement with an outside professional fiduciary company.*

The problem they had was that their current outsourced

arrangement was problematic and represented one of their largest remaining alligators. That's because this particular trust company they had partnered with was not in a preferred trust state. Worse, they were also poaching Jeff's best clients! So maybe the question was whether Jeff could find another professional fiduciary firm, in a preferred trust state, that wouldn't poach their clients?

Once Jeff came to this realization and brought it back to his business partner, they both realized this meant good news: their third partner, the one who'd had to pull out, would be able to come back as well. *Not* becoming a trust company meant he could have the time he needed to dedicate to his family. Deciding to *not* change meant the three business partners wouldn't need the huge capital infusion or the time commitment they thought would be required from each of the partners if they became a trust company.

So the threesome was re-united, a win-win-win solution!

From there, they took various meetings, all arranged by the trusted outside consultant, with a select group of professional fiduciary firms in preferred trust states. Within a few months they had signed with a new trust company in a preferred trust state, who also agreed not to poach their hard-won clients.

A happy ending all around! And not least for the consultant, who, as we saw in this story, was able to use his informal, indirect influence to strategically overcome the inherent limitations of Jeff's formal authority.

What *are* those inherent limitations?

As leader of his existing firm, Jeff is responsible for making important decisions and ensuring the overall success of the organization. His formal authority, however, comes with blind spots. In particular, we see in this example how Jeff's focus on raising capital and trying to establish a new trust company caused him to overlook certain crucial aspects of the business plan.

For one, Jeff had a blind spot in his inability to see the potential fiduciary risks and challenges that come with obtaining a trust license. In fact, he was so focused on achieving this narrow objective—of being granted a trust license—that he failed to fully comprehend what it meant to actually run a trust company and comply with all related requirements! This blind spot is significant, of course, because it could have put the entire venture at risk. Not only that, it could have harmed Jeff's current clients who rely on his existing business and services.

Finally, we see in Jeff's example how his formal authority limited his perspective and prevented him from considering an alternative solution. He became so fixated on the plan he had in mind, and so determined for it to succeed, that he couldn't even see there might have been other effective approaches. This blind spot was an invisible threat for Jeff and his firm at this point because he believed the need for a trust company was a fact.

In the story, we also saw how these blind spots could have led to disastrous results if it weren't for the informal intervention of the consultant.

The consultant knew he was merely an outside adviser who held no direct responsibility. It wasn't his place to make business decisions *for* Jeff. What he did have, however, was Jeff's trust in him and the ability to informally influence Jeff to participate in the workshop. Through that participation, Jeff was able to shed his blind spots—allowing him to see the Invisible Threat that might have scuttled the entire business.

Furthermore, what the consultant had was the informal authority rooted in his own expertise, combined with the trust he'd previously earned from working with Jeff in the past. And because the consultant wasn't bound by the same formal constraints as Jeff, he was able to offer alternative perspectives and ideas without undermining Jeff's formal authority.

Unlike for Jeff, or anyone with formal authority, a consultant has the freedom to think outside the box and consider unconventional solutions, solutions that Jeff or other leaders with formal authority would likely be blind to. As we can see from the story, it is through the consultant's subtle informal influence that Jeff is able to reach his *own* realization about the gaps in his business plan—and uncover the win-win solution for the Invisible Threat he'd been unable to see.

To put it another way, the person with informal authority provides the opening which then leads indirectly to the discovery of a viable solution not initially apparent to the person with formal authority.

For us, as consultants, learning to leverage the power of informal authority was crucial for helping various professional fiduciary clients who had been struggling in the wealth management industry. We started to realize this was the unseen ingredient that could help propel leaders with formal authority, leaders who were being held back by inherent constraints so couldn't see the invisible threats preventing their organizations from achieving better outcomes.

By tapping into one's expertise, credibility, and ability to build trust, while also respecting the organization's formal leadership, those with informal authority can become catalysts for adaptive change, guiding their organizations through the complexities of its adaptive challenges.

For readers of this book, we are hoping to spark the same kind of change within you. By showing how informal authority can bring about what may seem like minor miracles, we encourage you to draw upon the same indirect informal networks within your professional fiduciary firm to spark an adaptive revolution.

Informal authority is not just a tool, but a mindset shift—one that embraces questions over answers, why over what, growth over comfort, and collaboration over hierarchy. In the same way that Joanne's informal authority in her family continues to be fueled by the trust she built with her siblings, and the way that informal authority for consultants is fueled by the trust built with clients, you too can lean on the trust you've built in your organization to join together with other internal stakeholders (or even some external ones, such as auditors and examiners who you may still look at with a mixture of fear and apprehension) to collaborate and harness the collective power of your informal authority toward a breakthrough.

INFORMAL AUTHORITY IS A MINDSET SHIFT—ONE THAT EMBRACES QUESTIONS OVER ANSWERS, WHY OVER WHAT, GROWTH OVER COMFORT, AND COLLABORATION OVER HIERARCHY.

FROM TRUST TO COLLABORATION

What happens when those with informal authority within a fiduciary organization join together like this?

They start to tap into new resources, shed blind spots, clear the fog surrounding Invisible Threats, and come up with unconventional approaches to innovation, collaboration, and problem-solving.

Those with informal authority will realize they can take matters into their own hands and begin to do what's needed to close the gap.

To be clear, none of this means going rogue or agitating against formal authority. Rather, it's about working with the people inside your professional fiduciary firm to align everyone with the organization's goals and needs to strategically remove invisible threats on the path ahead. And the way you do this is through collaborative decision-making, as we'll see in the following chapter.

LEVERAGING INFORMAL AUTHORITY

1. FORMAL AUTHORITY VS. INFORMAL AUTHORITY

Standard Approach and Outcome:

- Rely on formal authority and hierarchical power to drive change and make decisions.
- Example: The Manhattan bank president's failure to effectively implement adaptive change due to reliance on formal authority alone.
- Outcome: Limited success in addressing adaptive challenges and potential resistance from those affected.

Counterintuitive Approach and Expected Outcome:

- Leverage informal authority, derived from expertise, credibility, and relationships, to influence and guide adaptive change.
- Example: Outside consultant guides Jeff through workshops and leverages informal influence to help Jeff see flaws in his business plan and discover a viable solution.
- Expected Outcome: Greater success in navigating adaptive challenges and fostering collaboration and innovation.

2. DIRECT AUTHORITY VS. SUBTLE INFLUENCE

Standard Approach and Outcome:

- Use direct authority and explicit commands to enforce change and solutions.
- Example: Outside consultant's initial reluctance to tell Jeff directly what to do, recognizing it would not be effective.
- Outcome: Simply telling people what to do and expecting them to follow.

Counterintuitive Approach and Expected Outcome:

- Use subtle influence and indirect guidance to help individuals come to their own realizations and decisions.
- Example: Joanne guides her siblings to complete household chores and avoid upsetting their mother to maintain family harmony.
- Expected Outcome: Greater acceptance and ownership of the adaptive change process.

3. QUICK FIXES VS. LONG-TERM ENGAGEMENT

Standard Approach and Outcome:

- Focus on quick fixes that address immediate problems without considering long-term implications.
- Example: Consultants providing immediate technical solutions without addressing underlying adaptive challenges.
- Outcome: Temporary relief but recurring issues and missed opportunities for growth.

Counterintuitive Approach and Expected Outcome:

- Commit to long-term engagement that involves addressing root causes and fostering continuous learning and adaptation.
- Example: Joanne develops trust and deep understanding with her siblings over the years, leading to sustained family cohesion and mutual support.
- Expected Outcome: Sustainable progress and long-term success in navigating complex challenges.

CHAPTER 6

COLLABORATING TOWARD A BREAKTHROUGH

NOW THAT YOU'VE COME TO APPRECIATE THE POWER OF informal authority to spark adaptive change, you need to understand *how* this important process comes about—and what specific actions you will need to take. In particular, we will show you how to leverage your unique ability as an informal authority to *provoke*.

Provoke?

Granted, it may sound like a brash word for us to use here, but the concept we're putting forth in this chapter is not a rebellion against formal authority. Rather, we're talking about provoking certain changes in your environment, removing certain obstacles, all toward preemptively setting in motion the adaptive solution needed.

When obstacles are removed, the river of growth and success can begin to flow once again.

That's because, piece by piece, you're getting rid of the things that aren't working. And it's all still happening within the general guidance of your organization's formal authority. You're using your informal authority, and collaborating with others in this informal role, to move the rest of the company (or an individual) bit by bit in the direction of adaptive change.

You're focusing first on injecting small changes, ones that your company's formal authority will undoubtably support, no questions asked. Then, from there you build on what you've started, continuing to nip away and remove ever greater obstacles. You're collaborating with others in the firm who hold informal authority, sharing diverse ideas, and starting to see the dividends of this wide-ranging discourse.

We love when this happens. And the best part about it is how, gradually, the adaptive capacity of the whole group increases. Together, you're able to effect greater change. New ideas are facilitated, leading to bigger breakthroughs ahead.

In this light, provoking is really just another way of saying "creating the environment you want." It's not about waiting for explicit permission from a formal authority. It's about realizing you have to spark change somehow.

So you just do it. You just start.

You leverage your informal authority to intentionally raise the stress level within your professional fiduciary firm. You use your unique influence to provoke action and create a sense of urgency and pressure. This then has the effect of motivating others to address issues, implement improvements, and drive change within the organization.

If adding more stress sounds like the *last* thing you need right now, we get it. But it is, in fact, just what's needed for creating urgency. When any system becomes unstable, it triggers a pressing situation that leadership must resolve quickly and not let linger.

In this scenario, the person who injects stress, a.k.a. the provoker, uses their reputation and informal influence within a company to act like a thermostat and raise the temperature on issues in the work environment. They increase (or conversely, lower) the heat depending on the importance of the issue and the team's ability to handle it.

How often does this approach succeed? If the provoker has a strong reputation and the team is resilient, their actions to raise the heat on a challenging situation can and often does lead to a breakthrough. But not overnight. To move toward such a breakthrough, a number of things need to happen. First, the provoker must adjust the pressure in the work environment by deliberately introducing or increasing stressors within the team or organization. They may do this by challenging the status quo, pushing for higher performance standards, or pushing the team into an adaptive challenge. The provoker's intent is to create a sense of discomfort or urgency that motivates individuals (or the team as a whole) to push their limits and challenge their way of knowing. By doing so, they provoke innovation, creativity, and growth, and set the stage for skillfully resolving whatever situation they've landed on.

THE PROVOKER'S INTENTION
HERE IS TO CREATE A SENSE OF
DISCOMFORT OR URGENCY THAT
MOTIVATES INDIVIDUALS TO PUSH
THEIR LIMITS AND CHALLENGE
THEIR WAY OF KNOWING.

From there, once a valid issue or dilemma has been identified and provoked, it becomes the responsibility of those with *formal* authority to take action and essentially convert the ensuing stress into productive work that will ultimately reduce the stress level. They do this by allocating necessary resources, drawing attention to the problem, and establishing a decision-making process. As for this last piece, a big of part of setting up and putting such a decision-making process in place involves the holders of formal authority having to consider the presence and relevance of conflicts, as well as how to manage them. Leadership must also decide on the best approach to decision-making—whether it be rational, intuitive, collaborative, etc.—based on various factors such as the type of challenge, the firm's resilience, the severity of the problem, and the available time to respond.

In cases where the problem and solution are known, it becomes a technical challenge, and leadership can make decisions rationally or intuitively. But in the face of an adaptive challenge—i.e., one where problems and solutions are unknown and buy-in and commitment are required from stakeholders—it is highly beneficial for leadership to adopt a collaborative decision-making process that aims to harness collective intelligence, diverse perspectives, and consensus building, as well as the potential resolution of conflicting viewpoints.

In this collaborative process, decision-making responsibility is delegated to assorted stakeholders who are then placed directly in the dilemma at hand—a dilemma that may well have been caused by their own reluctance to challenge their assumptions (about values, behaviors, and beliefs) in the first place.

Ideally, this collaborative decision-making process can then lead to what is called an "optimal conflict," where the professional fiduciary firm is pushed to the edge of its knowledge. This conflict then serves as a catalyst for resolution and innovative breakthrough. We'll return shortly to the concept of optimal conflict and how it inspires such breakthroughs. But first, let's dig deeper into what we mean by "breakthroughs."

The title of this chapter is "Collaborating Toward a Breakthrough" and what we are really describing here is the process of achieving significant progress in resolving the adaptive challenge. To be clear, this breakthrough may not necessarily yield an elegant solution to the dilemma. It could simply involve enhancing the team's adaptive capacity by:

- strengthening their resilience
- embracing discomfort
- resolving conflicts
- setting ambitious goals beyond their current comfort zone

This collaborative approach is key to gaining traction and making substantial strides toward successfully addressing the adaptive challenge, as we'll see in the following story of Joanne's time at law school.

PROVOKING AN ADAPTIVE SOLUTION IN LAW SCHOOL

JOANNE: If I hadn't provoked change in my environment and taken preemptive action to collaborate toward a breakthrough— if I had instead continued to rely on my usual approach to dealing with challenges—while I probably wouldn't have flunked out of law school, I would have been sorely tempted to come up with a plausible rationale for why it was better for me to drop out. Or even if I'd decided to stick it out, while I would have gotten my law degree—being stubborn enough to at least scrape by rather than acknowledge defeat and quitting—I would not have achieved the success I did and would have been miserable the entire time.

From the very start of my time at UIC School of Law in downtown Chicago, I wondered if I had made a huge mistake in thinking I could pull off this law school thing.[16] For starters, I felt like I was twice the age of everyone in my classes. In reality, the age gap wasn't quite as big as I imagined. But it had been decades since I'd attended college, and I felt out of touch with the latest technological educational tools. To give you some idea, in my very first class, Property Law, I was proud of myself for just having managed to locate the classroom and find a seat, and was excited to get the class outline so I could figure out what the course would be about. My excitement turned to a growing horror, however, as I looked around and saw that almost everyone around me had a big red textbook on their desk with "Property Law" stamped in gold on the front. From where I sat, I could even see that some people had tabs in the book and what looked like notes on their desk. Did I miss a class? I wondered. Then, it got even worse. The professor walked in, called out a student's name at random, and asked them to outline the first case. Immediately, a young woman stood up and, with confidence, read from her notes, providing a succinct summary of the case—a case I had no idea I was already supposed to have read! For the next eighty minutes I sat in abject fear that my name would be called. There were seventy students so the odds were in my favor. Nevertheless, I thanked my lucky stars when the class ended and I hadn't been called.

From there I bolted to the library, a sanctuary for me since childhood, to find a quiet spot to sit and pore through the reams of orientation information I'd received from the school, trying to figure out what I'd missed. There it was: a link I should have spotted before. When I clicked on it, I saw the classes I'd signed up for, including the one I'd just sweated through, plus a writing class, which was just two hours away, and a Contracts Law class the next day. In addition to the location and time for each, I saw the list of required textbooks and the assignment list for the semester, including reading assignments due that very first day of class.

How did I miss that link? I could have kicked myself. But my immediate concern was to get my textbooks ASAP. Rather than embarrass myself by asking a fellow student where to buy them, I waited until there was no one else at the library help desk, then sidled up to quietly inquire if there was a place I could purchase textbooks.

There was. Barely two hours later in my writing class, not only did I have the textbook in front of me, I'd also managed to speed-read my way through the assignment. While I wasn't confident about the material, at least I didn't feel as idiotic and stressed-out as I had that morning in Property Law.

On a side note, some years later I happened to watch a popular movie that had been out for a while—*Legally Blonde*. During the scene where Elle Woods is in her first law school class, completely unprepared as I'd been, I just sat and cringed. Maybe it should have cheered me up to see I wasn't the only person in the world who'd ever shown up unprepared for law school. But watching the film only made me feel foolish all over again.

Truth be told, it seemed like a small miracle that I had made it to law school in the first place. There had been so many hoops to get through. My initial challenge was to find a school in the area that offered a part-time program, which I needed to make the whole thing work with my job obligations. Then, there was the matter of how I would pay for it. Thank God I got a decent enough score on the LSAT to be granted a scholarship.

Before I had begun to pursue any of those things, I'd just assumed the law school ship had sailed. It's not that I didn't want a law degree. I just didn't think it was in the cards for me anymore, though I sometimes wished I'd gone to law school years before, instead of business school. In fact, when I was getting my MBA, I would often look with envy at the law students on campus, wondering to myself, *Why didn't I do that instead?* I even entertained the idea of doing joint law and MBA at the time, but I just didn't have the money.

So, it was a big deal that I had finally made it to law school. Part of the requirement for my scholarship, however, was that I get grades in the top third of my class. I also had to remain in the top third each semester or I'd forfeit the remainder of the scholarship. So I panicked when I got the results back from my first quiz. Out of seventy students, I had come in second to last! This was in Contracts Law class, taught by Professor Jones, who announced, as he handed back the graded quizzes, that anyone who scored less than 20 percent had to make an appointment to see him. I felt like a dismal failure.

Two days later, at the appointed time, I stood outside Professor Jones' open door, waiting for permission to enter. He saw me but didn't say anything, just kept typing on his computer. I assumed he was finishing an email or something so waited for him to finish and turn to me. After a few minutes, he still hadn't said anything. So I tiptoed in and slid onto the visitor's chair. Still typing, he asked, "Why are you here?"

"You said to make an appointment if we scored less than 20 percent," I stammered.

To that, while still typing but not yet looking at me, he repeated, slower this time, "So, why are you here?"

I realized he might have no idea who I was—he still hadn't even looked at me—so I put it more bluntly: "I failed the Contracts quiz. On my paper you said mine was the second lowest score." Then I waited for I knew not what.

Professor Jones was a tough professor, I'd already learned.

He'd been a former Marine, and it showed in the way he ran his class. If a student wasn't in the classroom when Professor Jones walked in, always precisely on time, they'd be locked out. During the second week of class, a student who was a minute late tried to get a fellow classmate to unlock the side door so he could slip in unnoticed. It ended badly, with both students locked out of that day's class.

Then, one day during the fourth week of classes, with everyone in their seats chatting as we waited for Professor Jones to arrive, he announced his presence with a resounding slam of the door. The room was shocked into silence. All eyes were on him as he stepped up to his lectern. He was fuming, but no one knew why. He waited a moment, then proceeded to reprimand us on how embarrassed he had been coming down the hall to discover that all the noise—"it sounded like a party going on"—was coming from his classroom. He said if we were evidently so well prepared for class that we could party instead of sitting quietly in our seats reviewing our case outlines, then surely everyone he called on would be absolutely perfect in presenting and defending that day's assignment, right? Uh-oh. I was one of the students who had not yet been called upon to present in class and feared today was going to be my unlucky day. I waited for Professor Jones to call out "Ms. Eby." But the two words never came. Before I knew it, class was over. Spared once again.

As I sat in Professor Jones's office, however, I knew my luck had run out. I waited for him to tell me what a failure I was, mentally bracing for a scathing lecture and hoping he'd let me stay in the class. Instead, he just asked again, "Why are you here?" By then I was confused and asked if he wanted me to leave. He ignored this and barked out a series of rapid-fire questions.

"Do you do the class assignments?" he asked.

"Yes," I replied.

"Do you prepare outlines?"

"Yes."

"Did you study for the quiz?"

"Yes"

"Did you attend the review class?"

"No," I said. In my defense, he knew that already because I'd told him I had to go out of town for work the week of the review class. I could tell he wasn't happy about my missing it. But what could I do? My dilemma was to keep my job or attend the class. I had to go on the work trip, but I wondered if I had made a huge mistake.

"Did you get notes from the review class you missed?" he asked.

"Well, no."

At that, he finally turned to face me. "Are you in a study group?"

"Uh, no."

He raised his eyebrows and said, "You'd better find one," then turned back to his computer. I'd been dismissed.

I left his office feeling bewildered. It seemed I was getting mixed messages. During orientation it was made pretty clear to us students just how competitive law school was going to be. We understood that a sizable percentage of our incoming class of first year law students wasn't going to make it to graduation. And the speakers during orientation didn't let us forget it. One of them instructed us to look to the person on our right, then the person on our left, and realize one of us three students would not be there the following year. Someone even said we'd be wise to start thinking of our fellow students not as friends but enemies! Virtually all the speakers said something to this effect and I was left with the impression that the vibe at law school would be each student out for themselves. Yet Professor Jones, a person in a position of real authority within the institution, not only suggested but commanded I join a study group.

Professor Jones had been so disappointed in how our class fared on the first quiz that he announced he would give us a second quiz—something he told us with disdain he'd never had to do in his class before. I was determined to excel on the second quiz. I attended the second review class, studied diligently by reviewing all the materials and class notes, and overall felt quite prepared. Meanwhile, I worked extra hard on my assignments. I even asked a fellow Contracts student, who sat next to me in my writing class and, like me, seemed to be a loner, for a copy of her notes from that first review class I'd missed.

I thought I'd done all I needed to excel on the second quiz. But when I got it back, though I'd improved, my score was just at class average. I felt even more like a dismal failure. What was I going to do? I had worked so hard and all it got me was class average. My scholarship was doomed and if I didn't receive that money, I didn't know how I'd get by. I started to feel I was in way over my head.

After receiving the mediocre quiz result, I phoned Matt to share the news—and immediately lost it, breaking down in a flurry of tears and emotion. This is not my typical behavior. Matt was shocked. He tried to calm me down so he could understand what I was saying. Finally, I blurted out, "blatantly average," then burst into tears again. Matt tried to cheer me up: "That's great," he said, "What an improvement!" And in some ways, I guess it was. But all I could think about was how much effort I'd put into the class since the first quiz, how studious I'd been, and all I got was class average!

I was competitive by nature, though I usually tried to hide that side of me, so I found myself in a dilemma where I didn't know what to do, how to battle through. Matt suggested I reach out to his business partner, a lawyer who had written my recommendation letter when I'd applied to law school. So I called her and, wouldn't you know it, proceeded to break down in tears all over again. After she calmed me down, I asked why she hadn't warned me about how hard law school was? She laughed and explained that if she had told me the truth I might not have gone through with it. She also reassured me that if anyone could do this—succeed in law school and keep my scholarship—it was me.

As sweet as she was to give me such a supportive pep talk, I wasn't fully convinced, but it did help. Something was changing in me; I was starting to feel fired-up. Getting that average score lit a spark in me. I told myself that if I was going to do this law school thing at all, I needed to rise to the challenge and knock it out of the park.

Easier said than done, though. Would I have what it took? Up to this point, I had basically been applying the same old Joanne playbook to my law school endeavors, the same methods I'd used successfully as a student in the past, through college and MBA school. Based on the miserable results I'd achieved so far in law school, however, something had to change. I didn't want to just get by. More than anything, I wanted to prove to Professor Jones that I truly belonged in his class.

I went to my student counsellor for help. She offered to transfer me to another Contracts class, confessing that she knew how tough Professor Jones could be. I was tempted, but also conflicted, and turned it down. As I explained to her, I needed to be able to learn from any professor, even the tough ones. I couldn't control how professors teach, but I should be able to control how I learn from them, regardless of their style. The truth, though, was I just couldn't let Professor Jones get the better of me. He'd provoked me that day in his office. And I was starting to realize this might have been his intent all along.

I confided in my counsellor that I needed to figure out how to be a student again, given the decades since I had last been one. Were there better ways of learning, new methods to get up to speed on? She gave me some articles about being a law school student. She also asked if I'd used any of the audio or visual materials in the library to help with the core curriculum subjects, like Contracts Law. No, I hadn't. So, as soon as our meeting was over, off I went to locate them. I borrowed some audio recordings and on my commute home that day listened to a Contracts lecture.

And it was on that same commute the following day, while waiting on the platform for my train home, that I spotted a girl who sat two rows behind me in Contracts class. After we both boarded, I moved through the crowd and got into the same car she was in, then sat across from her. I'd always been inherently shy, but, desperate to understand how to be a student again, I took this opportunity to talk with someone who looked fresh out of college. I pushed myself out of my comfort zone and smiled at her. She smiled back, and before I knew it we were chatting. Her name was Bethany. Over the course of that train ride I shared with her how badly I'd been struggling in Contracts class.

She was incredibly nice and said she'd been struggling too. Then she mentioned that she and two of her friends had started a study group, just the three of them. She asked if I wanted to join.

Did I ever? I thought, reminding myself of how much was at stake. Staying in the top third of my classes, in order to keep my scholarship, was no joke. And law school was not some kumbaya scenario where every student could get straight A's. No, it was simple math: with a bell curve in place for the core curriculum classes, for me to be a winner someone else had to be the loser. Or in my case, two people out of every three had to be losers for me to retain my scholarship! I'd learned from Bethany that not only was she on the same scholarship track as me, she'd discovered many other students in Professor Jones' class were too. I couldn't believe it: we were all competing for the same pot of funding. No wonder we got the toughest professor in the school. I was not looking like a strong competitor so far: out of two quizzes, one was an abysmal failure and the other blatantly average. I needed to turn things around pronto.

I realized I had to provoke a change in my environment. Professor Jones didn't just tell me I "could" join a study group, he'd pretty much commanded me to do so. This was an opportunity I needed to grab.

I also realized that Bethany and I had more in common than having the same commute home and being on the same scholarship track. We were alike temperamentally: she had the same hunger and drive to succeed that I did. She'd been a former national water polo player for Greece, no less! We both knew intuitively that being able to collaborate—to share our struggles and provoke each other to do better as we rose to the adaptive challenges of law school—would strengthen our resilience, collectively and individually. Law school students weren't allowed to actually team together, in the sense of divvying up class assignments or sharing outlines, unlike my experience in MBA school where we'd had to do just that to build teamwork skills. But Bethany and I knew that joining forces through a study group would help us embrace the hardship of law school, while also setting more ambitious goals that, as a collaborative group, somehow didn't seem so unattainable.

Over the weeks leading up to finals, we collaborated to swiftly institute a number of adaptive changes. Bethany and I realized the things we'd done as students before, the ways we'd operated, were not sufficient in this challenging new environment. In fact, all four women in our study group had to make adaptive changes, each in our respective approaches.

In my case, I had to make two adaptive changes. For one, I'd still been trying to keep up with all the normal things I used to do, the quotidian tasks like laundry, grocery shopping, yard work, and so on. I realized that those normal and necessary day-to-day things, as I thought of them, were in direct conflict with my ambitious goal of being in the top third of my class. So I faced a dilemma: keep my normal life and don't attain my goal, or adapt my environment to achieve my goal. The inconsistency hadn't registered with me before, but now I could see clearly: If all I wanted was those normal things, I would never have gone to all the trouble just to get into law school. Having made it there, however, those normal things were clearly in conflict with my law school goals. I realized I had to stop; raking leaves and the like could wait. School had to be my top and only priority; I couldn't get distracted. Around this time, I even started carrying around a Post-it note on which I'd written a Piet Hein quote I'd recently come across: "He that lets the small things bind him leaves the great undone behind him."[17] It helped remind me that I couldn't let small things like laundry and yard work distract me from my ambitious law school goal.

I felt vindicated, rather than discouraged, two weeks before Thanksgiving when Professor Jones delivered these dour instructions to the class: If we were to have any hope, he told us, of making the grade in our upcoming finals, which began the week after the holiday, there could be no distractions. He said something in class that day I've never forgotten: "There are no friends, there is no family. There's only eat, sleep, and study— and not necessarily in that order." A memorable mantra from an ex-Marine. He also went into specifics, spending a good half hour outlining exactly what he believed we should and shouldn't be doing to prepare for finals. What struck me most as Professor Jones talked and I took notes was how much his recommendations dovetailed with the recent changes I'd already made since meeting Bethany and joining the study group.

When I got home that night and told Matt I couldn't go to his sister's house for Thanksgiving, repeating what Professor Jones had told us about no friends and no family, he didn't argue. He saw my determination and knew there was no stopping me. (He was even nice enough to bring home a plate of food and piece of pie for me.) Matt was right: I was indeed filled with a new determination.

I had been testing various changes to my law school approach, and for the most part they were working. Collaborating with the study group had shown me just how much I needed to adopt new ways of learning. For example, I had already been listening to the audio tapes and made the change to doing so not only during my commute, but at any spare moment when I could be killing two birds with one stone—like when I was walking the dogs. Admittedly, some of the learning tools I encountered during this time, like the video lectures, felt foreign to me as someone of a different generation, but I tried them all—then adopted those that were the most effective.

Bethany and the other two women in the study group didn't struggle like me with modern learning tools—being much younger they were familiar with these technologies—but they had their own habits that needed to change. One positive habit they eventually adopted was to turn off their cell phone when they were studying. Being older and less screen-addicted, I already did this out of instinct, which they found strange. Whenever we studied together, they'd noticed I kept my phone in airplane mode and tucked out of sight in my bag. It was quite the contrast with the three of them, who checked their phones constantly and even had live video chats on their laptops during class and while studying.

I have a vivid memory of how Bethany came to the awareness of how much more focused studying she could get done when she put her phone away. She and I had gone to a library close to where we both lived, just the two of us this time. We arrived mid-morning and planned to study until dinner time. As we got settled, putting our coats, books, and bags into study cubicles across from one another, Bethany told me she was going to try turning off her phone like she'd seen me do. With that, we each settled into our studies. A few hours later (or so it seemed), we felt two taps on our shoulders. It was the librarian. We each looked up, puzzled at being disturbed, and removed our earplugs so we could hear her. "You have to go," she said. "We're closing." Shocked, we asked why they were closing early. She laughed and pointed at the clock on the wall. To our astonishment, it was already eight o'clock, closing time and well past dinner. Everyone else in the library was gone. Immediately, we reached for our phones. Bethany knew her mom would be frantic and I was afraid Matt would be worried too. I was going to call him when we got outside, but he was already there waiting in his car. With relief, Bethany and I hopped in, thanking him for being there. Matt laughed and shook his head, saying he'd figured my phone was off and, knowing the library would kick us out at closing time, thought we'd welcome the ride. Did we ever. Dizzy from concentration and lack of food, neither Bethany nor I could believe we'd just put in a solid ten hours of concentrated study!

How do you think things turned out for me and Bethany? How effective were the adaptive changes we made?

I'm happy to report that our early collaboration led to breakthroughs that first semester, and endured through our entire law school years, during which we were able to achieve further, almost continuous breakthroughs. We did this by consistently bringing about the distinct adaptive changes that we each needed to succeed. Ultimately, it was through this approach that Bethany and I both made our higher-education dreams come true. As for our two study-group pals, they also made the adaptive changes they needed to succeed, and both have gone on to excel in their chosen careers, one a top executive for a large corporation and the other a professor at the same law school!

Speaking of professors, what about Professor Jones, the person who set this collaborative journey in motion for me? He remained in the picture as my Contracts professor, provoking me to learn all I could from him, and not just in that first semester class. When I showed up in his second semester class, he couldn't believe it. On the first day of class, while doing roll call, he couldn't hide his surprise when he came to my name. He stopped, looked at me, then said in front of the whole class, "Ms. Eby. You. You're back for more?" I stood up, which we were required to do whenever he called on us, and said, "Yes, Professor," then sat back down. I was secretly pleased he'd been so surprised. Yes, we'd gotten off on the wrong foot the first semester, and I can't say I was a shining star in my first Contracts class, but I was determined to show him what I was really made of, which was why I'd enrolled in his second semester class, against the advice of my counsellor. I knew, as did the others in my study group who'd also enrolled in his second semester class, that the adaptive changes he was provoking in us were important in ways that went beyond just getting a passing grade.

The four of us soldiered on, learning as much as we could from Professor Jones—mostly about contracts, but also about how to approach challenges in school and even in life—and we were all the better for the experience.

As a side note, on the last day of that second semester, I was in the elevator when it stopped and in walked Professor Jones. It was just the two of us and he looked at me, saying, "It's you." When we got off on the first floor, he turned to me and said, "You did well this semester. I didn't think you would." He told me that over the past few months he'd talked to the others in my study group and they'd mentioned to him how good I was at helping them stay on track, like I was the "mom" of the group. He then raised his eyebrows, smiled at me and reached out to shake my hand. "Well done," he said, before walking off. Hard to describe the emotion I felt when he grasped my hand; on my commute home I felt like I was floating on air. I'd done it—through collaboration with my study group, I'd achieved a real breakthrough!

While each of us in that study group had our own challenges, the biggest problem we all needed to fix was the gap between how we wanted our law school experience to go and the grim reality of the first-year law school experience before our group came together and we started to collaborate. Halfway through that first semester, there seemed to be an insurmountable gap between what we each had—our current reality—and what we wanted to have.

However, by collaborating to embrace the adaptive challenges head on, we were each unquestionably successful in closing the gap. For me, not only did I make the Dean's list and keep my scholarship through law school, I won another scholarship, achieved a few academic awards, and graduated *cum laude*. I would be remiss to not also mention a happy ending to this story as it relates to my personal life. One of the most memorable moments of my life was during my commencement and seeing the proud smile on my son's face when I walked past him on my way to the stage as they announced those scholastic achievements.

KEEPING UP WITH THE JONESES

Joanne's law school story has many interesting facets but one of the most important takeaways is how she and her friends were able to grow their adaptive capacity, a crucial trait for becoming successful attorneys—and one knowingly cultivated in them by Professor Jones.

In taking up his invitation/exhortation to form study groups, they opened themselves up to the intense physical and mental discomfort that comes with the territory in law school: think fierce competition, immense workload, and relentless pressure to excel. This is also precisely how they found their drive to adapt. Embracing discomfort allowed them to develop the discipline they needed to prioritize efforts, manage time efficiently, and make sacrifices to achieve their goals.

The expanded adaptive capacity of Joanne, Bethany, and the others meant they became better at pushing through difficulties. Professor Jones understood this and harnessed his position to help cultivate resilience within his students. He knew that resilient individuals have a special ability to see challenges as opportunities for growth and learning; moreover, they demonstrate emotional strength, enhanced ability to embrace the unknown, and a positive outlook, enabling them to navigate adversity with confidence and agility. Above all, Professor Jones recognized that the ability to withstand stress and recover from difficulties is integral to the kind of robust work ethic that drives lawyerly success.

Lawyers, much like professional fiduciaries, are problem solvers. Professor Jones saw how the study groups compelled law students to confront complex concepts, grapple with challenging issues, and engage in rigorous debates. This process also honed their analytical skills, enabling them to consider multiple perspectives and develop persuasive arguments. Moreover, he saw how the emotional demands of the study groups fostered greater emotional intelligence. Students learned to manage stress, handle conflicts, and empathize with clients and colleagues—skills vital in navigating the legal profession with empathy, professionalism, and resilience.

But what Professor Jones really sought to cultivate in Joanne and his other students boils down to the way they approach *conflict.*

In the legal world, a realm defined by dispute and disagreement, addressing conflicts head-on is of course critical to success. But what Professor Jones was trying to draw out of his students is something more specific and interesting. His concerns were threefold: (1) seeking, (2) provoking, and (3) resolving conflicts.

1. **Seeking Conflicts:** In study groups, students actively engaged in debates, discussions, and legal challenges. This engagement broadened their knowledge, honed critical thinking skills, and enhanced their ability to advocate effectively for clients.

2. **Provoking Conflicts:** By questioning the status quo and proposing alternative solutions, students became catalysts for positive change, contributing to the evolution of adaptive practices. In them we see how provoking conflicts in a controlled and constructive manner helps to challenge existing norms and principles, stimulating intellectual growth and innovation.

3. **Resolving Conflicts:** Professor Jones knew that effective conflict resolution requires all of the following: identifying common ground, negotiating agreements, and finding mutually beneficial solutions. Among his students, he encouraged communication, empathy, and an understanding of all parties' interests and motivations. Armed with these skills, many

went on to become skilled negotiators and mediators, facilitating win-win solutions without needing litigation.

All in all, we see how Professor Jones cultivated a never-ending resolve in his students to set and reset ambitious goals beyond their comfort zones.

The resolve Matt witnessed Professor Jones set for Joanne and those in her study group reminded him of a quote from Dr. Eli Goldratt, creator of the mermaids/alligators/pots of gold/crutches change matrix. As it happens, Matt was lucky enough to attend one of the last Viable Vision seminars given by Dr. Goldratt himself, and got to hear him say his infamous line, "If you think you can achieve your goals on your own, you must not have set them very high." Dr. Goldratt was all about people and companies setting audacious goals for themselves.

IF YOU THINK YOU CAN
ACHIEVE YOUR GOALS ON
YOUR OWN, YOU MUST NOT
HAVE SET THEM VERY HIGH.

This book is about professional fiduciary firms, not law schools, but we've spent time on this particular story because it is such a rich sandbox to explore these ideas. Law school is a crucible for analytical thinking and problem-solving. Through tackling intricate legal cases and engaging in rigorous debates, students like Joanne build resilience in problem-solving. They learn to break down complex issues, consider multiple perspectives, and develop effective strategies. Just as important, law school offers an opportunity to build a robust professional network. Interaction with classmates, professors, and legal professionals teaches students the value of collaboration, support, and mentorship. In turn, this network reinforces their resilience, offering a vital support system, valuable advice, and growth opportunities.

It was through these very methods and experiences that Joanne and the other students found themselves placed smack dab in the middle of the grand adaptive challenge that is law school—in other words, right where Professor Jones wanted them, fertile soil for pushing them to question their values, beliefs, and behaviors.

BUT WHAT HAPPENS WHEN THERE'S NO FORMAL AUTHORITY AT ALL?

The SECURE Act (which stands for Setting Every Community Up for Retirement Enhancement) was signed into law in December 2019, followed in quick succession by the SECURE 2.0 Act of December 2022. The SECURE Act and SECURE 2.0 Act brought substantial changes to the retirement account rules that had been in place for decades. The primary objective was, of course, to encourage more Americans to save for retirement, but these new laws contained significant retirement-related changes with many highly technical details.

We bring this up here because, as many readers are aware, those laws didn't come with much guidance for professional fiduciary firms or other firms on the securities side of the wealth management industry. The law's complex changes have confused taxpayers and plan sponsors alike, according to Kelley Taylor in a recent article on the SECURE Act 2.0, and it's those same taxpayers and plan sponsors who look to service providers in the wealth management industry for help when triggering events occur, such as reaching retirement age, leaving an employer-sponsored retirement plan, or inheriting a retirement account from a loved one.[18]

To illustrate the confusion, look, for example, at the impact these changes have had on inheriting an individual retirement account (IRA) from a loved one.

The Employee Retirement Income Security Act of 1974 (ERISA) protects the assets of millions of Americans so funds placed in retirement plans during their working lives will be there when they retire. ERISA is the federal law that sets minimum standards for retirement plans in private industry.[19] Meanwhile, the Treasury Department's Internal Revenue Service (IRS) is responsible for the rules that allow tax benefits for both employees and employers related to retirement plans, including vesting and distribution requirements.

For decades, the rules published by the IRS associated with IRAs had few changes. While the IRS puts out annual updates to its guides for use in preparing tax returns, for the most part these updates were minor.[20] The major elements for inherited IRAs had not changed much. There were two classes of beneficiaries—spousal and non-spousal—and while the rules were not exactly simple, and required precision to ensure compliance, service providers in the wealth management industry, including custodians and trustees, had well-developed policies and procedures in place that outlined the rules for both spousal and non-spousal beneficiaries, including qualified trusts as beneficiary.

That all changed with the SECURE Act. Considered the most impactful retirement plan legislation since the Pension Protection Act of 2006, it included major changes that impacted nearly everyone: recent retirees, employers, full and part-time employees, financial advisors, IRA custodians, and IRA trustees.[21] Among the complexities wrought by the changes was the need to maintain two classes of inherited IRA beneficiaries after January 1, 2020—those who inherited pre-SECURE Act and those who inherited post-SECURE Act.

For IRAs inherited post-SECURE Act, the ability to stretch payments from inherited retirement arrangements over a lifetime was no longer permitted for most non-spousal beneficiaries. Instead, a ten-year payout rule required all funds to be distributed no later than December 31 of the tenth year following the date of death of the decedent. And both conduit and accumulation trusts fell under the new payout rules.

Ed Slott, a well-regarded tax and IRA expert in the wealth management industry, had this to say about the SECURE Act's impact on inherited IRAs:

> Before 2020, if you inherited an IRA and you were a designated beneficiary named on the beneficiary form, an individual, you could do what was called a stretch IRA, an extended deferral, take RMDs over your life expectancy based on your age. You could defer that out for 20, 30, 50, 80 years. Congress didn't like that. They thought it was too big of a break. They killed that in the original Secure Act and replaced it with basically a 10-year window. In other words, they're saying, "Look, beneficiaries, the party is over, all of these funds have to come out by the end of the 10th year after death." It was effective for deaths—or if you want to put it a nicer way, inheritances—in 2020 or later.[22]

Then came 2020, COVID-19, the CARES Act, and its impact on required minimum distribution rules for IRAs, including inherited IRAs.

Finally, with the December 2022 passage of the SECURE 2.0 Act, though the new measure was intended to expand and enhance the SECURE Act, the resulting complications made it seem more like the straw that broke the camel's back.

For players in the wealth management industry, existing policies and procedures needed to be updated, everyone needed to be educated and trained in the new requirements, and the IRS needed to publish rules and tax guidance for the new laws. It all seemed too much. Even industry experts such as Ed Slott, who are typically looked to for guidance in the way of educational webinars and other training sessions, didn't have all the answers since the legislation had gotten way ahead of the rules and formal guidance. In the words of Christine Benz from *Morningstar* when interviewing Ed Slott in a recent segment, "People have questions, questions, questions."[23]

For those who were in the industry when the Gramm–Leach–Bliley and Dodd–Frank legislation was passed, this might all feel like déjà vu, with complex laws being enacted without a comprehensive overarching regulatory framework for players in the industry to rely on to ensure they are doing the right things for their clients.

The IRS recently delayed implementation of required minimum distribution final rules—yet again.[24] While the IRS has also waived penalties for missed distributions, making for a total of four years in a row with waived penalties (2021, 2022, 2023, and 2024), that does not solve what remains a serious issue in the industry. If the IRS has yet to finalize its rules, that means players in the industry, particularly professional fiduciary firms who are trustees of trusts that have inherited IRAs during that time, and also IRA custodians and financial advisors trying to help their clients, lack clear guidance—from formal authority—around how to distribute those inherited IRAs to the ultimate beneficiaries. While it might seem tempting, a professional fiduciary firm cannot simply say to, for example, the adult children and grandchildren of a recently departed loved one, that they just have to wait for their inheritance until the IRS finalizes its rules. So the industry is caught in a weird kind of limbo.

In the world of wealth management services, the firms themselves have no formal authority when it comes to inherited IRAs and have always looked to the IRS for formal guidance. Before the SECURE Act, the rules had been the same for decades. It was (relatively) easy-peasy. With the new laws, however, there is industry-wide disarray over inherited IRAs with nowhere to turn if the IRS itself cannot provide clear guidance.

Compare and contrast this situation with the recent enactment of the Anti-Money Laundering Act of 2020 (AML Act), which became law in January 2021. The Corporate Transparency Act (CTA) was one part of the AML Act and included major legislation that requires most US entities to report beneficial ownership information to the Financial Crimes Enforcement Network (commonly known as FinCEN).[25] At first, it didn't seem there would be much, if any, impact for the wealth management industry. Most players already had to comply with a previous rule, the FinCEN CDD rule, and the CTA just seemed to require that the business owners of those entities provide information to FinCEN. As time went on, however, it gradually dawned on those who provided corporate trustee services—professional fiduciary firms—that there might, in fact, be requirements they needed to understand and comply with. In direct contrast to the lack of clear guidance from the government for complex inherited IRA rules, however, FinCEN has taken its responsibility as the formal authority over all things to do with the Anti-Money Laundering laws very seriously.

A quick glance at FinCEN's home page (www.fincen.gov) will take anyone right to the information they need. A professional fiduciary firm can click through a few links and see every rule published under the AML Act and the CTA, including the new Beneficial Ownership Reporting Rule and accompanying Beneficial Ownership Information Reporting requirements. Furthermore, instead of providing just a single publication of their Frequently Asked Questions (FAQs), FinCEN has kept those FAQs current by continuously updating them with answers to more and more questions, including whether a trustee of a trust that owns an entity must file a beneficial ownership information report.

Which takes us back to the overarching question: what can a professional fiduciary firm do when there is no formal authority to guide appropriate action? In this scenario, one choice is to provoke action, to create that sense of urgency and pressure in that will motivate others to collaborate toward a breakthrough solution.

Ignoring the situation is not an option. We have seen too many professional fiduciary firms struggling with all the unknowns around the lack of formal guidance from the IRS for complex inherited IRA situations. At a recent wealth management industry conference we attended in May 2024, with various experts in a breakout room—representatives from professional fiduciary firms, top legal counsel, skilled tax professionals, and more—the stress was palpable when it became clear there was still no formal guidance around complex inherited IRA situations. To be fair, it was not a complete vacuum of information. The IRS has done a great job trying to publish as much guidance as they can, but even a government agency can only do so much. In the most recent update to Publication 590-B, for example, which outlines rules for distributions from IRAs, you'll find under the section involving *applicable multi-beneficiary trusts* the following "tip" from the IRS: "You may want to contact a tax advisor to comply with this complicated area of the tax law."[26] (Wow, you don't say?) But in the breakout room at that conference, everyone could see that the guidance from the IRS was insufficient and that professional fiduciary firms, in particular, faced with whether and how they should distribute inherited IRA assets, were struggling with complex inheritance questions, without anyone in the room able to stand up and definitively state, "Here's your answer!"

Naturally, no one in the breakout room, some of whom were, in fact, tax advisors, wanted to make a definitive statement without being able to rely on formal IRS guidance. Everyone there was looking for answers, but no one had them.

What can a professional fiduciary firm even do in a situation like this? First, they are required to use their fiduciary lens to see who the ultimate beneficiaries are for those inherited IRAs. In the simpler scenarios, sub-trusts can be established to hold correct percentages of an inherited IRA, and over the next ten years the beneficiaries of those sub-trusts would receive their fair share. But what of the more complex situations? An IRA that had been inherited by a non-spouse beneficiary, for example, when the non-spouse beneficiary subsequently died without naming future beneficiaries. Or any inherited IRA involving multiple beneficiaries, particularly where the class of beneficiaries are different or the dispositive provisions vary among them.

There is not yet a perfect formal solution provided by the IRS, and this chapter in no way intends to provide technical tax or legal advice, but we have learned of, and participated in, a number of small groups and networks across the wealth management industry that came together informally to collaborate. While none of these groups have formal authority when it comes to inherited IRAs, their very existence is evidence that a new environment has emerged in the industry, and with it a need for an adaptive solution.

The jury is still out as to where this is all going to lead and what professional fiduciary firms will be able to come up with. One possibility, however, is that some of those firms may choose to have their legal counsel apply to the IRS for special rulings, which, if approved, could set precedence and itself become the authority to support collaborative decision-making from within the industry.

We don't know yet if this informal collaboration we've observed among the various groups and networks will create a breakthrough solution. But there's something inspiring about how, even in this very complicated and frustrating situation with no easy answers, many in the industry are finding ways to at least attempt to provoke a change in the environment and trigger an adaptive solution—one that will benefit many.

Moreover, in this particular situation with the IRS and inherited IRAs, the industry really had no choice, having reached the limit of its collective knowledge, but to collaborate and try to achieve a breakthrough.

It had reached the point of what is called optimal conflict.

WHAT IS OPTIMAL CONFLICT?

Have you ever been in a situation where applying some pressure led to positive change?

If not, you're probably wondering: *Can this really work? Is it actually helpful to add more stress, considering how stressed everything already is?* The answer is yes. As we mentioned at the top of this chapter, targeted stress can indeed, surprising as it may seem, create the urgency needed for adaptive change. By intentionally increasing the pressure, you highlight the urgent issues that require immediate attention.

Let's dig into this process a little further. When a system becomes slightly destabilized, leadership must address the issues promptly, converting the added stress into productive work to resolve problems. This process is akin to adjusting a thermostat: raising the temperature highlights important issues, and lowering it eases the pressure to prevent the system from becoming overwhelmed. This strategic manipulation of stress leads to breakthroughs by pushing teams to stretch beyond their comfort zones.

Still struggling with this concept and how you can use it? If so, let's try the following experiment. Pause for a moment and think of a time when a significant challenge in your work environment led to creativity or innovation.

Okay, hold that thought. Turning our attention back to the idea of the optimal conflict, remember that this refers to the point where you can no longer apply existing knowledge and must find new solutions. It is a state of being that fosters growth and innovation by pushing teams to the edge of their comfort zones. Creating optimal conflict also involves raising the heat on issues within the organization, sensitively pressuring individuals to stretch their limits creatively and strategically.

It's not about causing chaos but introducing Structured Discomfort that leads to adaptive change. The goal is not only to intensify the issue, but also to transform these stressors into drivers for innovation and growth.

Now, think about how it played out in your case when you faced that significant challenge in your work environment. Did the tension or conflict lead to a breakthrough?

We know from the beginning of this chapter that, in the face of adaptive challenges where problems and solutions are often unknown, collaborative decision-making becomes essential. This process harnesses collective intelligence and diverse perspectives by engaging stakeholders directly in problem-solving. Put this all together and you see how collaboration among informal leaders can create an environment conducive to breakthroughs, combining strengths to tackle complex issues.

We see this in Joanne's law school story about how working within the study group showed her the power of adapting and collaborating. At the start of her law school journey, she felt overwhelmed and out of place. Her turning point came when Professor Jones, a tough but respected figure, insisted she join a study group after she'd received a failing grade and had to meet one on one with him. During that meeting, Jones questioned her preparation and pretty much commanded she find a study group. This was out of character for Joanne, who always preferred to work independently in her studies.

After that difficult conversation, Joanne took his advice. Rather than give up, she adapted. She found a study group with classmates who were also struggling. By pooling effort, supporting one another, and overcoming the adaptive challenges of law school by adopting new methods of learning, and living, they started to excel, achieving breakthroughs.

Being in a collaborative study group made all the difference. The targeted stress took them out of their collective comfort zone and the added pressure of being in the group forced adaptive change. They shared organizational skills, discussed cases, and explored new learning tools. Through their collaboration, they not only survived but thrived in the pressure of the competitive environment.

One pivotal moment—when Joanne and Bethany, engrossed in study at the library, realized they'd lost track of time and studied straight through dinner—helped them see they'd adapted. Their intense focus and mutual support became the norm, paving the way for their success.

Joanne's story is a great illustration of how conflict can lead to breakthrough, and how the path toward it runs through collaboration.

Do you see the same pattern in your work story?

ACHIEVING COLLABORATIVE SUCCESS
AS A PROFESSIONAL FIDUCIARY

Faced with the SECURE and SECURE 2.0 Acts, wealth management firms have been able to provoke action internally and create adaptive solutions that might later become the industry standards. Experts like Ed Slott have highlighted this shift, noting that where Congress curtailed tax deferral benefits, firms had to respond quickly to new realities, reshaping how advice is given and services are provided, despite, or perhaps because of, the lack of formal authority. As wealth management firms grapple with the ongoing challenges and the slow pace of regulatory guidance, they exemplify the critical role that adaptive change plays in maintaining client trust and compliance.

This proactive approach to a vastly changed regulatory environment is a vivid demonstration of how firms can transform a regulatory challenge into an opportunity for leadership and innovation. But it also shows how the industry as a whole can lead, not just in response to but in advance of formal guidelines, and through these key principles of collaboration and adaptive solutions, as follows:

- **Informal Collaboration:** The various groups draw on the distinct power we see in this kind of collaboration to tackle complex issues effectively, even without formal guidance to set the standard.
- **Adaptive Solutions:** Working together, these groups create adaptive solutions essential in uncertain environments, where problems and solutions are by definition unknown.

We witnessed both of these in action at the recent industry conference. We also discussed in this chapter the importance of seeking, provoking, and resolving conflict, all of which will align well with any adaptive challenge. In fact, this method ensures that professionals in *any* field can develop the skills needed to succeed. But you have to keep exercising those muscles, and a good way to approach that is to:

1. **Seek Conflicts:** Encourage active engagement in debates and discussions to make both sides of the dilemma visible. Look for assumptions.
2. **Provoke Conflicts:** Challenge norms and principles to stimulate intellectual growth.
3. **Resolve Conflicts:** Use win-win methodology to keep relationships intact. Win-lose will end up lose-lose in the long term.

In professional fiduciary firms today, especially within the current, broader wealth management landscape contributing to the Invisible Threat, robust problem-identification and problem-solving abilities are greatly needed. Remember: with challenges that are adaptive, *both* the problems and solutions remain undefined. By embracing discomfort and collaborating informally, ultimately you will be well poised to achieve the breakthrough results necessary for success.

Not only that, but you will develop resilience, as well as a strong work ethic. Identifying and resolving conflicts through adaptive solutions will also significantly enhance your team's adaptive culture.

As you move forward along your journey, we'll call on you to reflect on all you've learned in this chapter—namely, the power of adding controlled stress to provoke necessary changes, the importance of collaborative decision-making in addressing adaptive challenges, and the concept of optimal conflict as a driver of breakthrough solutions. Think about how you can integrate these principles to create an adaptive, resilient, and innovative environment.

The next chapter will push further into embedding adaptive change into your organizational culture for sustained success.

COLLABORATING TOWARD A BREAKTHROUGH

1. USING INFORMAL AUTHORITY TO PROVOKE CHANGE

Standard Approach and Outcome:
- Follow formal authority and established protocols to initiate change.
- Example: Relying on formal decisions and directives from leadership to address issues within the organization.
- Outcome: Controlled, incremental change within risk appetite and tolerance.

Counterintuitive Approach and Expected Outcome:
- Leverage informal authority to provoke changes in the environment, creating urgency and pressure to drive adaptive solutions.
- Example: Individuals use their reputation and informal influence to raise the stress level and motivate others to address pressing issues.
- Expected Outcome: Accelerated innovation and adaptation to changing circumstances.

2. CREATING STRESS TO FACILITATE CHANGE

Standard Approach and Outcome:
- Minimize stress and maintain stability within the organization.
- Example: Avoiding changes that could disrupt the current work environment or increase stress levels.
- Outcome: Comfort and stability, with risk controlled and application of technical solution.

Counterintuitive Approach and Expected Outcome:

- Intentionally introduce or increase stressors to create a sense of urgency and discomfort that drives innovation and growth.
- Example: The provoker uses informal influence to challenge the status quo and push the team into adaptive challenges.
- Expected Outcome: Enhanced adaptive capacity and ability to tackle complex challenges.

3. OPTIMAL CONFLICT AS A CATALYST FOR BREAKTHROUGHS

Standard Approach and Outcome:

- Avoid conflict and maintain harmony within the organization.
- Example: Suppressing conflicts to maintain a peaceful work environment.
- Outcome: Superficial harmony and unresolved underlying issues. May have resistance undertone.

Counterintuitive Approach and Expected Outcome:

- Seek, provoke, and resolve conflicts to push the organization to the edge of its knowledge and capabilities.
- Example: Creating Structured Discomfort and optimal conflict to drive innovation and growth within the organization.
- Expected Outcome: Breakthrough solutions and significant progress in resolving adaptive challenges.

CHAPTER 7

CREATING AN ADAPTIVE CULTURE

Y OU'VE PROBABLY HEARD THE SAYING, "CHANGE IS THE only constant in life," as Greek philosopher Heraclitus famously put it. Change pushes us outside of what's familiar, known, and expected, making it uncomfortable for many. Well, it's time to get comfortable with being uncomfortable because nowhere is this truer—change pushing us outside of the familiar—than in today's fast-changing, post-GLBA era of trust and wealth management. And when everything around you seems in constant flux, the big question becomes: How can you and your organization stay relevant?

The answer lies in creating an adaptive culture.

But here's the thing: adaptive change isn't just about being flexible or responding to change as it comes. It's about pushing yourself and your organization beyond the boundaries of what's comfortable or familiar. It's about accepting the unknown and setting goals that feel almost impossible—goals so audacious that they force you to break through your existing limitations.

IF YOU'RE NOT MEETING EXPECTATIONS, RAISE THE STANDARDS.

This approach goes against the grain of what most of us are naturally inclined to do. We're wired to play it safe, avoid risk, and set manageable, incremental objectives. But as Dr. Eli Goldratt would say, the times when you're struggling the most are the times you need to raise the bar even higher and shoot for the stars. Why? Because when you aim for something so big that you can't achieve it on your own, you're compelled to collaborate, innovate, and adopt a mindset that's open to the unknown.

But before you can foster this kind of bold adaptive change, you need to take a hard look at what's holding you back. For many professional fiduciary firms, the biggest obstacles are internal—rooted in frustration from applying technical solutions to adaptive challenges and a reluctance to step out of the comfort zone. This is known as inertia.

Another major hurdle is the focus on stability over flexibility. Organizational systems want to maintain equilibrium and keep things steady; after all, stability brings a sense of control. But if you're overly focused on maintaining the status quo—on getting good audit reports or avoiding regulatory scrutiny—you could be missing out on the bigger picture. Leaning too heavily on what's safe, instead of exploring what's possible.

Then there are those silos, the departmental barriers that keep teams isolated and prevent the kind of cross-collaboration that's essential for innovation. When different parts of your organization are not talking to one another, they can't share ideas, and they certainly can't work together to achieve those audacious goals required to break through.

But here's the good news: it does not have to stay this way. By challenging your comfort zones, encouraging collaboration, and rethinking how you approach risk, you can start removing these obstacles and build a culture that's not just adaptive, but audaciously so.

So, how do you do it? What's the process? You already know from reading the prior chapters: Use your informal authority to challenge these assumptions. This creates pressure that provokes adaptive change toward a breakthrough. Then, in order to break through, you'll need to collaborate. Lather, rinse, repeat—these are the initial steps needed to create an adaptive culture.

A CULTURE OF ONGOING IMPROVEMENT

MATT: Back in Chapter 3, I told you about my lifelong weight-loss journey and how—after years of being stuck in the up-thirty/down-thirty pattern—I finally entered the gate and embraced an enduring, adaptive solution. Not only did I lose one hundred pounds, I also changed my whole lifestyle and have been a different man ever since.

Before achieving this adaptive change, I had been struggling with a problem, a gap between what I wanted out of my weight-loss attempts and what I was actually getting, which was that I seemed to always yo-yo back to where I had started. At a certain point, I started to feel like there was no way out of this vicious cycle. Somehow, in my mind, I had established an artificial limit: yes, I knew how to shed thirty pounds and could do it over and over again, but I couldn't see past this frontier. It represented the boundaries of my existing knowledge.

When I reached that point of optimal conflict where I could no longer apply existing knowledge and had to find new solutions, I knew I couldn't escape the bitter truth: my old knowledge about weight loss was insufficient for overcoming my dilemma. I had to break through my own limitations.

Initially, my breakthrough had been inspired by the woman in my Weight Watchers meeting who had lost one hundred pounds. But it's also worth mentioning that, around this same time, I had been working with Dr. Goldratt, already introduced in earlier chapters as the creator of the change matrix, who is also author of the popular and influential business management book, *The Goal: A Process of Ongoing Improvement*.

Dr. Goldratt had no clue I was using ideas about business constraints and how to alleviate bottlenecks from *The Goal* and applying them to my own goals around weight loss. In fact, I don't think I ever talked about my going to Weight Watchers or anything like that with him. But he was the inspiration for so much.

I remember one time we were at a conference, and he asked the conference attendees the question, what do you do if you're not achieving your goals? His answer was counterintuitive: he said that when you're struggling with what you set out to accomplish, that's when you need to raise the bar even higher and shoot for the stars. His logic was that, by aiming for the proverbial stars, when you then end up only hitting the moon, you'll still have performed so much better than you ever expected.

That's what I did when I raised my goal to losing one hundred pounds. But what was really going on was I was challenging my underlying assumptions. Shooting for the stars meant I would have to break through my limited knowledge and totally change the way I operated. I got this from Dr. Goldratt. But it wasn't the only thing he taught me. There was something else, something very important and relevant to this chapter and to this stage in your own journey: he said that when you reach the point where you realize you have to break through, you'll need to collaborate. You can't do it on your own. In fact, he explained, if you think you can pull it off solo, then something must be wrong: you must not have raised your goal high enough.

He insisted on what he called Audacious Goal-Setting—not only in the sense of the goals being way outside your normal comfort zone but also far beyond what you could ever hope to accomplish on your own. By committing to such a bold goal, you'd have no choice but to collaborate with others and together build a new path forward.

This is where the idea of an adaptive culture comes in.

In my case, first I knew I had to enlist Joanne. I asked her to help me track all my food. One time I even called her from an out-of-town business meeting: I was at a restaurant and didn't know what to order. She went online, looked up the menu, then texted me with what was safe for me to eat within my new health guidelines. Together we collaborated on my weight loss journey.

This internal adaptive culture Joanne and I began to create actually grew outward from there when we started sharing our success story with others at Weight Watchers meetings—and helping them shift their mindset toward adaptive change.

The whole philosophy of Weight Watchers is adaptive. They're not offering a technical solution; their program is not a diet. Instead, it's about a mindset shift, adapting who you are in order to change underlying habits. As with all adaptive change, it's not about fixing a particular problem. If it were, it would only require a technical solution. But instead, whether we're talking about Weight Watchers or a trust company, an adaptive solution is about fixing the person, or people, having the problem.

TECHNICAL SOLUTIONS ARE ABOUT FIXING THE PROBLEM; ADAPTIVE SOLUTIONS ARE ABOUT FIXING THE PERSON HAVING THE PROBLEM.

To bring this all full-circle, taking everything I learned from Dr. Goldratt about assumptions and audacious goals, and everything Joanne and I tried to do using our informal authority in supporting the adaptive culture at Weight Watchers meetings, what it adds up to is precisely what we have carried with us over the years at Nth Degree.

It's all part of the same adaptive solution. We help our clients see and challenge their hidden assumptions and blind spots. We show them how their dilemma has ripened to the point where they're at the edge of their knowledge, in a state of optimal conflict, and must break through. Finally, we call upon them to establish an adaptive culture, so they can make these kinds of changes on an ongoing basis—an approach Dr. Goldratt called POOGI, which stands for a Process of Ongoing Improvement. You can think of this process simply as continuously striving to do better, even if just a little at a time. Just one percent better is an improvement, as they say at Weight Watchers!

This is the way you and your professional fiduciary firm can maintain viability and relevance in today's fast-changing environment. You must instill this adaptive culture throughout your entire organization, breaking down silos and fostering cross-departmental collaboration.

BRINGING IN THE FORMAL LEADERSHIP

But where do you start? How exactly do you go about fostering an adaptive culture, integrating new practices, instilling new values, beliefs, and behaviors, and overcoming resistance to change?

By removing those obstacles we talked about at the beginning of the chapter, venturing beyond your comfort zones, and enabling cross-departmental collaboration.

And by, finally, bringing in the formal authority.

What was needed *before* was something very different, a kind of unofficial collaboration and discourse among the informal leaders within your company—all toward, first, identifying common goals, and then, influencing and provoking the adaptive change you seek. But what's needed, at this level, is for formal leadership to step in. That's because it's the organizational culture that's changing. And you can't change the culture of an entire organization without buy-in from leadership.

From there, once you have that buy-in, you'll be surprised at how well things start to fall into place. For example, it's at this very juncture, just when you've increased transparency and begun to promote more effective communication, that you will see exciting interdepartmental collaboration start to emerge.

What happens overall is that by removing one obstacle, another will start to come loose, then another and another. As departments become less siloed, with each no longer trying to work and fix problems in isolation, you'll see a common language begin to take shape. And once you have that top-down formal authority to support the efforts, you'll encounter less fear and resistance among the other employees just coming into the new adaptive environment.

Then, you'll observe how, especially with professional fiduciary firms, who deal so much with the Invisible Threat associated with acceptance of fiduciary risk in the wealth management space, a new understanding will develop around that risk as something not to be afraid of but rather a positive—a potential asset to the overall organization.

These broader organizations will start to see that high-risk accounts can actually carry a high degree of value and can be great accounts for the skilled professional fiduciary firm to accept. We're not talking here about taking on risk for its own sake, but rather accepting a level of fiduciary risk that becomes an asset for the organization—that is, once it realizes such business is not inherently bad. Quite the opposite. But it does require that crucial change in mindset: first, from wanting to steer clear of such invisible threats altogether to, then, being willing to see through the fog a little and consider whether to accept these high-risk accounts to, finally, having the fog lift and becoming genuinely good at accepting and servicing such business—no longer considered unacceptably *risky* business.

It brings us great satisfaction when we see this happy evolution play out with clients, especially because we understand how challenging it is for professional fiduciary firms to master fiduciary duties and make the adaptive change in this way.

CREATING AN ADAPTIVE CULTURE IN A PROFESSIONAL FIDUCIARY FIRM

To help guide you on how to cultivate an adaptive culture within a professional fiduciary firm, you can use the following framework:

1. **Assess Hidden Assumptions:** Identify and challenge the hidden assumptions responsible for the existence and persistence of silos. Determine how these assumptions shape values, behaviors, and decision-making processes.

2. **Acknowledge Silos:** Identify existing silos within the organization. Recognize how these silos hinder communication and collaboration.

3. **Promote Cross-Departmental Collaboration:** Create initiatives to encourage interdepartmental projects. This can be in the form of cross-functional teams working on common goals or regular interdepartmental meetings to share insights and knowledge.

4. **Leadership Commitment:** Get buy-in from leaders at all levels to ensure they are committed to promoting adaptive change. They should model adaptive behaviors and be visibly engaged in adaptive practices.

5. **Foster a Learning Environment:** Invest in continuous learning and development programs. Encourage employees to pursue ongoing education and training that will keep them updated with industry changes and innovations.

6. **Encourage Risk-Taking:** Create a safe environment where employees feel comfortable taking calculated risks. Recognize and reward innovative ideas even if they don't always succeed.

7. **Implement POOGI:** Adopt Dr. Goldratt's Process of Ongoing Improvement methodology to facilitate continuous improvement. Regularly review processes and practices to identify areas for improvement and ensure ongoing adaptive change to continuously do better.

8. **Enhance Communication:** Improve communication channels within the organization. Ensure that information flows freely and transparently across all levels and departments.

9. **Align Goals and Vision:** Make sure all employees understand and are aligned with the company's long-term goals and vision. Instill a sense of purpose and direction that drives collaborative efforts.

10. **Evaluate and Adjust:** Regularly assess the effectiveness of the implemented practices and make necessary adjustments. Keep the adaptive culture dynamic and flexible to meet changing needs.

By implementing these steps, your organization can methodically remove barriers and build an adaptive culture. However, it's important to note that many organizations lean toward remaining in their comfort zone and resist changes that would help propel them forward.

STUCK IN THEIR COMFORT ZONE

There certainly wasn't much enthusiasm for change coming from a trust company we worked with who was, at the time, being asked to absorb a new book of trust business that accompanied an acquisition the bank holding company had just closed on.

In the trust industry, there are regulations that determine what capacity you can work in once you have your trust license. For example, in addition to accepting appointment as trustee of trusts, your organization *could* be a custodian for an account and just manage custody assets on behalf of the client. Or it *could* act as an investment manager and manage a portfolio of marketable securities for an investment management account. Neither of those two capacities are strictly fiduciary in nature (or rather, Fiduciary with a capital F) since there is no trust agreement. Instead, the services would be governed by the custody or investment management contract the client signed. Because you'll be limited by what you can do in those roles, such as acting only on the client's direction if you are custodian, as well as what you *cannot* do in other roles, such as self-dealing by investing in proprietary funds if you are investment manager, it's not uncommon in the trust industry that some professional fiduciary firms will elect to stick to just being a trustee for personal trusts and rely on its pre-acceptance process to weed out accounts outside of their current business model. This is a known and safe comfort zone for many professional fiduciary firms.

Similarly, many newly licensed trust companies, especially when just starting out, will at an organizational level stick to what they and their people know best. They'll say, this is how we built up our reputation and book of business—why would we want to change?

Fair enough, but what happens when their clients start asking for more? Which is what we saw in Chapter 3 when Mary's tax clients asked if she could step in as an individual trustee of special needs trusts for their children. This is part of the Invisible Threat across the wealth management industry. Having had a taste for the one-stop-shop service model that became popular in the post-GLBA era, clients in this day and age have come to expect it from any firm that operates in the wealth management industry, including those providing peripheral services such as tax filing.

If your professional fiduciary firm is already providing trustee services, it's common to hear someone say, "You're already the trustee for our trust, can't you also help manage our investment portfolio? We know it's not in a trust, but we just want you to manage our other investments."

We saw that happen in an abrupt way with the client we were working with. They did not want to, or plan to, broaden their services. They were skilled at providing high-touch personal trust administration services to their clients—grantors or beneficiaries of trusts—and outsourced the investment management of those trust portfolios. Imagine their dismay to learn that the new acquisition consisted solely of custody and investment management accounts, neither of which they were familiar with. They assumed it was too much of a different capacity for them, and they weren't sure they knew how to do it right.

It also wasn't so simple to just say no—it would jeopardize the entire deal and Corporate would not even entertain that notion. This caused more than a little internal tension.

The root of this conflict was competing incentives. The bank holding company entered the deal because of lucrative retail bank business it brought in, but the deal required that they accept the book of business from its trust department. From the corporate perspective, taking on those accounts was a no-brainer. Here was potentially lucrative business for the trust company, and the regulations allowed their professional fiduciary firm to accept custody and investment management accounts under its trust license.

From the trust administration team's perspective, however, taking on the new accounts meant they would have to figure out how to administer custody and investment management accounts that lacked standard trust provisions to guide their actions. They didn't want to accept the new business, even though it would increase their overall revenue.

For those on the trust company side, they believed the new accounts would also increase their fiduciary risk. They knew they *could* take on this new kind of business since their trust license permitted it. But they weren't confident in their ability to properly manage this new business. Not only were the account types unfamiliar to them, the new book of business came with some staff from the acquired bank who would be making the investment management decisions—something the trust company had always outsourced.

This is a common dilemma. Not necessarily with those same

circumstances, but where a professional fiduciary firm, skilled in one area or aspect of the trust business, is pressured by the larger wealth management organization, or by their own current client base as we saw with Mary and those special needs trusts. And we get it: the last thing you want to do as a professional fiduciary firm is wind up in the crosshairs of examiners, or worse yet, stuck with a regulatory civil monetary penalty (like a South Dakota trust company we heard about at a recent conference[27]) because of what you can't see, the Invisible Threat of the fiduciary risk under the surface of that new business.

But it doesn't have to be an either-or situation. There is a third way between pursuit of growth or revenue and an overabundance of caution that leads to missed opportunities.

The path we're referring to is the same one we've been talking about through this chapter, the adaptive path, where you remove internal obstacles so you can move forward with confidence, collaboratively within your adaptive culture, into new business areas.

WHAT LIES ON THE OTHER SIDE

When internal obstacles are removed, and a true adaptive culture is developed and nurtured, professional fiduciary firms start to see the fiduciary landscape for what it really can be and come to accept that change is constant.

They start to challenge long-held assumptions and beliefs. Often, once challenged, they can't even remember where a particular assumption or belief came from in the first place. They just accepted, or were convinced, without proof, that something was true for so many years and made so many important decisions based on those long-held institutional assumptions or beliefs, such as avoiding custody or investment management accounts because they were too risky, that they never thought to revisit them. They stuck to the same script even though their ability to manage the fiduciary risk could already have changed over their years in the business.

The funny thing is, the original assumption or belief may very well have been true at the time they established whatever rule they put in place. By embracing an adaptive culture, however, the organization will start to realize that their old rule—driven by their institutional assumptions or beliefs—may no longer be necessary or valid. Why not? It's because the situation will have changed over time, or the technology will have improved, and the original assumptions or beliefs can be challenged. Then, if they no longer hold true, they can be formally invalidated, allowing the organization to move forward on a different path.

Yes, it is difficult to challenge assumptions and beliefs. But it's a lot easier when formal leadership supports the change process. Not only can they display a true commitment to change but also be instrumental in providing the guidance and resources to drive this transformation across the organization and create an adaptive culture. When this happens—when internal obstacles like a lack of communication from leadership or among different departments are removed, and a true adaptive culture is developed and nurtured—what you get, what lies on the other side, is the glorious converse or mirror image of those things. With increased transparency, for example, comes more effective communication, better sharing of information across all quarters of an organization, and greater opportunities for adaptive change.

Ultimately, professional fiduciary firms able to successfully integrate these ideas and values into their culture come to realize that, while stability and control are important, they should not come at the expense of adaptive change. We saw that firsthand with our client. They collaborated with the newly acquired staff, accepted the new book of business, and even raised their goal by then asking themselves, *Why not use our new capabilities in investment management services for all our existing trust accounts, instead of delegating it to an outside manager?*—ultimately achieving a true win-win solution for the entire organization.

Stability and control are indeed important. But equally important, if not more so, to your organization's success are flexibility, adaptive change, and yes, acceptance of higher levels of fiduciary risk.

These values go beyond the workplace as well. Once you realize you can, and indeed must, continuously adapt and grow, you, the individual, become so much more of a complete person. You will marvel at just how limiting your original assumptions were, how trapped you were by your own built-in beliefs. And the very process of accepting these truths will make you stronger.

When your professional fiduciary firm, or you individually, have achieved adaptive success, there's no going back. Just like there was no going back for Matt after he adapted—not just losing weight, but adapting who he was as a new person.

But how do you ensure that the adaptive solution you've achieved is an enduring one? Are there invisible threats still lurking beyond your capability of seeing them through the lens you have?

CREATING AN ADAPTIVE CULTURE

1. EMBRACING RISK AS AN ASSET

Standard Approach and Outcome:

- Avoid risk to ensure stability and minimize potential losses.
- Example: Professional fiduciaries steering clear of high-risk accounts to avoid potential complications.
- Outcome: Stability but limited growth and innovation.

Counterintuitive Approach and Expected Outcome:

- View risk as a potential asset that can create value and growth opportunities.
- Example: Seeing high-risk accounts as valuable and becoming skilled at managing them effectively.
- Expected Outcome: Enhanced adaptive change and innovation and the ability to take advantage of lucrative opportunities for growth.

2. OVERCOMING INTERNAL RESISTANCE TO CHANGE

Standard Approach and Outcome:

- Maintain the status quo to avoid disrupting established practices and ensure job security.
- Example: Departments and business lines operating in silos and resisting initiatives that challenge their traditional roles.
- Outcome: Employee comfort but stagnant organizational culture.

Counterintuitive Approach and Expected Outcome:

- Challenge comfort zones and encourage cross-departmental collaboration to drive adaptive change.
- Example: Breaking down silos to foster collaboration and share goals across departments and business lines.
- Expected Outcome: Increased innovation and a dynamic, flexible organizational culture.

3. ENCOURAGING AUDACIOUS GOAL-SETTING AND COLLABORATION

Standard Approach and Outcome:

- Set realistic, achievable goals to ensure steady progress and minimize the risk of failure.
- Example: Setting modest goals that can be achieved independently without the need for extensive collaboration with other departments and business lines.
- Outcome: Predictable results but limited breakthrough achievements.

Counterintuitive Approach and Expected Outcome:

- Set audacious, ambitious goals that require collaboration and collective effort to achieve.
- Example: Setting high-reaching goals that push the organization to collaborate across departments and business lines and innovate beyond current capabilities.
- Expected Outcome: Significant breakthroughs and development of an adaptive culture.

CHAPTER 8

ENSURING AN ENDURING
SOLUTION

N CHAPTER 7, WE SAW WHAT IT LOOKS LIKE WHEN YOU
break through to an adaptive culture. This sets the stage for
what we're going to discuss in Chapter 8: how to achieve and
maintain the solution that's best for you and your organization.

How do you guarantee you don't fall back into your old
behaviors? How do you ensure that your solution is one that
endures?

First and foremost, it's about taking the adaptive success
you've had so far, and the adaptive culture you've built, and
making it part of your very identity. When professional fiduciary
firms start to identify in a different way and think of themselves
as problem-solvers, their entire brand changes. In a sense, they
transform into a completely different company.

This is possible for any organization. Say, you're in the
automotive industry. Maybe your company has traditionally
manufactured cars that run on fossil fuels but now you're pro-
ducing electric vehicles and thinking of yourself as a green

business. It's not just that you've made these adaptive changes to benefit the environment, but that the shift has adapted *what* you are, your very brand, your target market, and how you convey it through your messaging.

With an adaptive solution, you're not setting your sights on the problem itself so much as the person (or organization) experiencing the problem. This is often referred to in organizations as *changing the system*—not necessarily the technology system but all the general processes and internal mechanisms for what your organization does and how it operates.

The idea behind this concept of changing the system is that, if you and your organization are looking to build sustainable solutions, then you know that the changes you have to make will be at the system level.

This is important because, as we've seen throughout the book, not all changes are the *right* changes. A routine, technical fix, for example, is certainly not the right change if what you're looking to do is respond to complex shifts in your environment.

Or, as we pointed out in Chapter 4, "Every improvement requires change, but not every change is an improvement." Recognizing this important distinction and getting the right help to, in turn, identify the right change is what allows your organization to break through to an adaptive culture.

ADAPTIVE CHANGE
TRANSFORMS WHO *YOU* ARE.

And from there, what you'll find is that your adaptive success has become such a part of the fabric of your organization that it's seeped into its very identity, as an organization and its culture, and even as individuals within the organization.

Adaptive change is transformative: it changes who *you* are.

For Matt, it's not an exaggeration to say adaptive change transformed his very being, transformed the kind of man he is and how he moves through the world. He didn't even realize at first how much had changed, even just physically. It was Joanne who first noticed it.

HOW I GAINED A NEW HUSBAND

JOANNE: When Matt had his adaptive breakthrough, obviously he didn't lose those one hundred pounds overnight. But it didn't take long before I registered that something was different about him.

After shedding the first fifty pounds, there was a noticeable change in his speed and mobility when we went out to walk the dogs, something we'd always done together. I was typically a pretty fast walker; Matt, not so much. If I had to stop to tighten up my boot laces, for example, Matt would just keep walking, knowing I would quickly catch up to him.

I distinctly remember a day came when I stopped to tighten up my boot laces like usual but as I started walking again, I saw that Matt was way ahead and moving at an unusually brisk clip. I thought something was wrong and called out to him: "Matt, what's up? Slow down!"

He turned and gave me a confused look. "What do you mean, slow down?" he shouted back. "I'm walking the same pace I always walk!"

"No you're not," I huffed back at him as I hustled to catch up. "Why are you going so fast?"

He didn't believe me and thought I'd just taken longer lacing my boots. He literally couldn't tell that anything was different.

"I know what it is," I said. "You're probably using the same force as always, but because you're lighter, you're propelling yourself forward at a greater speed."

Matt just gave me his trademark look that said, better than any words could, I wasn't making any sense. We left it at that.

A month or so later we were hiking in a mountainous area near Las Vegas, on a pretty rigorous trail up and down the steep hills. We had attempted this hike once or twice before but had never managed to make it the whole way. This time, not only did we reach the end of the trail, but when we did, Matt shocked me by saying he wanted to continue hiking on another trail.

"Wow, okay," I said. This was very uncharacteristic of him, but I was happy to see Matt so fired up and full of energy. So, onward we trekked.

This time, I was the one struggling. When we reached the end of the second trail, Matt looked at me with a curious expression and asked, "What's with you? Why are you huffing and puffing like that?" If I hadn't been hunched over, elbows on my knees, trying to catch my breath, I might have been tempted to give Matt my trademark look that said, better than words could, he was on very thin ice.

Why was I huffing and puffing? The more appropriate question was: why wasn't he?

"Matt," I said, "I'm not the one who has changed. You have!"

He just gave me his look. We left it at that.

A few months later, after Matt had lost about seventy-five of those one hundred pounds, we were at the airport, about to get on a plane. Matt had just walked away to buy some water for the flight. So when I heard the announcement that passengers were boarding, I looked up and scanned the waiting area to see if he had returned. *Where's Matt?* I thought, he hates missing his boarding time. Then, all of a sudden, he was standing right in front of me, like he'd just appeared out of thin air.

"You're here!" I exclaimed.

He looked at me strangely. "Yes," he said. "I was walking right toward you, didn't you see me?"

Turns out he had even been waving his arm, trying to get my attention. But I had been looking for the old Matt, the seventy-five-pounds-heavier Matt. And so when his figure appeared, it was so visually different from what I was expecting that my brain must have played a trick on me.

"I didn't even recognize you!" I said. And it wasn't just his shape, it was also the way he walked. "I feel like I have a new husband," I told him. "I don't even know what you look like!"

That was the genesis of what became a standing joke between us, where I boast that I got a new husband without the inconvenience of a divorce. Even now, more than a decade later, it makes us chuckle.

It's actually more than just a silly joke. On the one hand, obviously we're being facetious. But on the other, Matt was indeed a changed man. He ate better, moved more, enjoyed outdoor activities that he'd never been able to participate in before. And naturally, he looked different. It wasn't just that he was so much thinner; he wore different clothes, stood taller, and again, even walked differently.

The transformation went way beyond just losing all that weight. It even went beyond the physical. He had expanded his horizons. His whole attitude toward life had changed.

Even our relationship had been strengthened in certain ways—like the fact that we could now engage in all these fun new pastimes together, from long hikes in the mountains to kayaking on lakes.

Not only had Matt embraced adaptive change; he'd transformed his life.

What began with him adapting his physical body had evolved into him taking on a totally different mental outlook. For one thing, I could see he recognized the importance of maintaining the great progress he had made. Unlike in the past, when he would lose weight and swiftly regain it, now it was like something had finally clicked and he understood this wasn't a one-and-done situation.

In the past, he had succumbed to the same pitfalls so many people do when they join a program like Weight Watchers. He had approached it like a diet, and after losing thirty pounds, thought he was cured.

Those earlier attempts had been strictly technical solutions, so it's no wonder the weight came back. After the initial success of losing thirty pounds, there was no adaptive change. Moreover, all he had really done, in executing the technical solution, was address the symptoms of the problem. He had made a short-term behavioral change by dieting, which was far from an enduring solution.

In order to achieve the enduring solution he needed, he knew he had to keep going to Weight Watchers. So he continued to attend the meetings and he started to give back, as he puts it, by participating in special sessions as a speaker to share his weight loss story, in the hopes of inspiring others to change not just their diet but their mindset. But even that formulation doesn't capture the scale of the change. It's bigger than a mindset shift. It's about adapting who you are, your very identity.

I know this is true because I saw it firsthand with Matt, day in and day out. Having been by his side through his whole adaptive journey—before, during, and after his breakthrough—I got to witness his remarkable transformation.

Matt had to recognize he was no longer the same person he'd been all his adult life. And having changed his physical environment in such a profound way, he also recognized there was no going back. In fact, he had broken through and adapted so completely that a return to his earlier status quo was really not even an option. Too much had changed. For instance, and this may seem like a trivial example, he was a hiker. Even if he were to regain some weight, hiking was now part of his identity. He was a hiker, therefore he hikes. How does one undo that?

Not that he would ever want to, but it's also just not possible. To this day, when speaking at those Weight Watcher meetings, he explains it like this: "It doesn't mean I'll never gain weight again—anything can happen—but I can't go back to the way I was before. That environment is completely gone."

I couldn't agree more. It wasn't just that Matt lost some weight. He became Matt 2.0—a complete reset. And he was proud of his new identities. Now he identifies, for example, as a person who buys clothes off the rack in the store, rather than having to order custom sizes like he used to. And he identifies as someone in good physical condition, who goes to the doctor proactively—for checkups, and to ensure his good health going forward—rather than going out of necessity because of high blood pressure or a heart problem.

Why is this so important? Because when you embrace positive new identities like this, it strengthens your resolve and solidifies your belief that you are indeed a different person. Above all, it gives you confidence that the adaptive change that fueled your transformation is going to last.

It's how you ensure that yours is an enduring solution.

A GOOD PROBLEM TO HAVE

For Matt, having had this lifelong weight problem and struggling to close the gap between his weight loss goals and his reality, then breaking through and achieving his adaptive solution, as well as doing the work to ensure sustainability, all adds up to what people in our industry like to call a "good problem."

When you have a good problem, it means you are facing the kind of dilemma that solves you before you solve it.

How does *it* solve *you*?

By revealing the limits of your thinking and driving you into that optimal conflict we described in Chapter 7.

A good problem, in this context, carries the power of transformation, because when you recognize that you're at those limits, specifically in the way you understand the solution, then you know it's *you* that has to change.

A good problem changes the very way you derive meaning.

Perhaps most of all, a good problem delivers benefits that transcend your original understanding of both the dilemma and the solution. Better yet, these benefits continue to grow and multiply over the course of your life, as you take what you've learned and apply it to other optimal conflicts you may pursue.

Another way to describe this is that the problem results in a *grasp that is greater than your reach*.[28] You reach to get a solution, and this reach is likely fairly narrow. But then, what you get out of it on the other side, what you ultimately grasp or take away, far exceeds the original reach.

But with all this talk of good problems and their benefits, the question then becomes: how do you keep this good thing going?

THE IMPORTANCE OF FEEDBACK LOOPS

We already saw how Matt's practice of giving back to his Weight Watchers community helped him ensure an enduring solution. More specifically, it provided an essential "feedback loop." In professional fiduciary firms, there are two fundamental tools for establishing these feedback loops.

One is the classic fiduciary risk assessment you may already be familiar with. When you've gone through the adaptive change and broken through the limits of your prior thinking and understanding, though, you'll see your results through a different lens. The low-risk items are your existing strengths. But the elements revealed as high-risk you will recognize as new opportunities. You can take advantage of them. Or not: you may not be ready, of course, but by having your risk assessment refreshed, at least every now and then, you can use it as a feedback mechanism toward maintaining adaptive success.

The other big feedback tool is the oft-dreaded annual audit. Professional fiduciary firms like yours are, of course, bound by regulatory requirements to have all their significant fiduciary activities audited each year. But you're not the same firm you once were. You have an adaptive culture and it's even become your new identity. So when you get that audit report, you'll see it not like a school report card, something you fear, as if you were in trouble with your teachers. Instead, you'll use it to your benefit, leveraging all the feedback it provides to ensure an enduring solution.

In some cases, the audit may confirm what you already suspected, that, yes, you are weak in operational controls or asset management areas. That information is helpful in itself. The audit may also reveal you're starting to slip in little ways you didn't realize—and inspire you to take action. Here's what you won't do, however, in the wake of an audit: panic and make bad decisions that only address the symptoms of the problem. Since you're a such different organization culturally than you were before, not only will you come to welcome your annual audit, you'll actually partner with the auditors to get the valuable information you need as you move forward.

DON'T FEAR YOUR ANNUAL "REG 9" AUDIT. EMBRACE IT FOR THE FEEDBACK IT PROVIDES.

Whether it's the audit or the risk assessment, you're using the feedback not to eliminate risk but to bring it out into the open. Recall our words from the Introduction: the Invisible Threat doesn't come from the risk itself, but from the not-knowing. To ensure your adaptive solution endures, you have to avoid falling back into that fog. That's why risk assessments and audits should be used for their valuable feedback-loop capacity. As an example, many larger financial institutions have entire in-house risk divisions whose job it is to update the risk assessments and provide reports of the results that are used by the organization as valuable feedback loops.

Before we move on from this discussion of feedback tools, let's touch on fiduciary risk assessments: though we believe our industry, ourselves included, have traditionally put too many of our eggs in this particular basket—which may have contributed to many of the hidden assumptions and beliefs we're trying to encourage you to challenge—nonetheless we still see risk assessments as one of many helpful tools for professional fiduciary firms.

That's why we welcome it when organizations we've worked with—and helped shepherd through their own adaptive change in the past—call us back for a tune-up of their risk assessment. It means they're thinking about their enduring solution in the right way. They understand that change is constant.

While a company that's truly achieved adaptive success and instilled it through their culture should theoretically, by definition, continue to adapt and see their solution endure, in practice we know it's not quite that simple.

After all, if change is a constant, as we've been saying throughout this book, of course that also applies to these businesses themselves and their personnel. Sometimes, what we see is that the company as a whole didn't adapt. Only certain key people did—and now those folks are gone. Or sometimes an organization just needs confirmation they're still on the right track, which it often very much is. Or maybe they just need our help with a little course correction. This is all still great: none of it means they failed in continuing to exercise their adaptive muscles. In fact, it's precisely because of their adaptive culture that they're able to see clearly when something changes in their environment and they are aware they need help with whatever new threat has emerged from the fog.

Point is, this is very different than thinking they're cured and going back to square one, culturally, with the same old cycles of blame and recrimination, the same hidden assumptions, and the return to the same old values, beliefs, and behaviors. Trust us, you don't want that to happen in your firm. That's why we believe it's important to take advantage of the feedback loops we've described, like Matt does with his giving-back routine at Weight Watchers, and as we encourage you to do in order to achieve an enduring solution.

THE JOURNEY NEVER ENDS

The value of these tune-ups really comes into focus when we look at the overall adaptive journey of the organization in question.

One of our longtime clients, for example, couldn't be more different now than when we started working with them over twenty years ago. When we were first called in, they did not even understand what "fiduciary" meant. That's because they had always outsourced this role to an outside professional fiduciary firm. After a certain point, they decided they wanted to do it themselves, so they got a limited power, state trust company license that permitted them to be their own trustee.

Problem was, after they got the license and in-sourced the trustee responsibilities, they didn't know how to perform the job of a fiduciary. So they just kept doing what they had always done before they had the trust license. Meanwhile, because they had already fired the professional fiduciary firm who had previously handled the trustee work for them, the trust accounts they had been so excited to administer just sat there. Nobody was paying any attention to them. The first time the examiner came through and saw that they hadn't been doing all the fiduciary activities they needed to do each year to keep up with trust regulations was a rude awakening.

That was when we got the call. We went in and conducted a fiduciary risk assessment. The feedback it provided showed them their highest risk was in the area of regulatory compliance. Not much of a surprise there, given they didn't even know what they were supposed to be doing under trust regulations. They were also exposed to a lot of what is called administrative risk, also no big surprise because they didn't even know what they were supposed to be doing with the trust accounts they'd been neglecting.

A rude awakening indeed. What happened over the years,

however, is that this company became incredibly adaptive and incredibly good at being in the trust business.

As recently as six years ago, for example, in recognition of the fact that the elderly matriarch and grantor of the trusts was not going to be around forever, they acted preemptively to adapt the entire governance framework of the firm to establish clear rules for oversight of future trusts, distributions, and disputes that might arise. They anticipated their environment was going to change, so they pulled us in to help—as they had previously over the years whenever they saw a major threat emerging.

That's the important point: even after building an impressive adaptive culture, they continued to pursue feedback and guidance. They would reach out to us to make sure there were no regulatory changes they'd missed, or learn about anything they needed to know, then they would adapt accordingly.

Could it be that this particular organization was just more adaptive, or at least open to adapting, all along? To an extent, yes. Even from that very first time we came in, twenty-four years ago, to conduct their first fiduciary risk assessment that alerted them to their regulatory and administrative risk, they didn't argue with us. Nor did they panic and scramble for a Band-Aid solution that would only fix the symptoms, not the problems. This alone put them ahead of the pack and gave them a head start in their adaptive journey.

They also demonstrated an ability to embrace the unknown in going out and getting their own trust license, because they did not know what exactly to do with it once they got it. (An audacious goal indeed, as Dr. Goldratt might have said.) And unlike many professional fiduciary firms, they never obsessed about or prioritized getting good exam and audit reports. They were always willing to accept the risk that even though they thought they were compliant, an examiner or auditor might interpret a situation differently. They were okay with that feedback and found it invaluable in making further adaptive changes.

So yes, there has always been something special about this firm and its organizational adaptive culture. But having been a client of ours from almost the very beginning of Nth Degree, we've seen how well they've continued to strengthen their adaptive culture over the years, through different generations of staff. Different people, same adaptive culture. Through it all, they've stayed on the offense, never abandoning their adaptive mindset toward ensuring an enduring solution.

It will come as no surprise to us, then, when the matriarch does inevitably pass away, this organization will be able to step up and handle the situation in exactly the way she will have wanted.

THE LIGHT AT THE END OF THE TUNNEL

Beyond the tune-ups and feedback loops, you'll know you've ensured an enduring solution when you and your professional fiduciary firm instinctively approach change by looking to the system level.

Moreover, you will know your solution is enduring when you can see that the adaptive changes you have implemented are sustainable as well as scalable, meaning you can apply them to other problems and get the same result.

That's because you'll have a trusted toolset you know you can draw from whenever you experience an optimal conflict.

You will be able to sustain your enduring solution and even carry it with you when your career and life take you to new places.

And what you'll see in the next chapter is how, personally, from within, you can help your professional fiduciary firm work through the tools outlined in this book to ultimately achieve its own enduring solution. This, despite the tensions of operating within the wealth management industry that you are probably all too familiar with: pressure from the Board and management, complaints from advisors and beneficiaries, ongoing regulatory changes, examiner and auditor expectations, staff turnover, and more.

Once you can *see* the Invisible Threats facing your professional fiduciary firm, you will have the lens needed to tackle them. You'll be able to help your firm develop its own adaptive culture—just like the professional fiduciary firm in the previous story—to ensure an enduring solution even when new invisible threats appear.

ENSURING AN ENDURING SOLUTION

1. ADAPTIVE SOLUTIONS TRANSFORM INTO TECHNICAL SOLUTIONS

Standard Approach and Outcome:
- Keep adaptive solutions separate from technical solutions, viewing them as distinct.
- Example: Maintaining adaptive solutions as ad-hoc effort without formalizing into standard procedures.
- Outcome: Limited evolution of adaptive practices into standardized operations.

Counterintuitive Approach and Expected Outcome:
- Recognize that adaptive solutions will evolve into technical solutions once they become repeatable and integrated into daily operations.
- Example: Matt's weight loss journey starts as an adaptive challenge and becomes a sustainable, repeatable health regimen.
- Expected Outcome: Sustainable practices that were once adaptive challenges become routine technical solutions.

2. FEEDBACK LOOPS AS TOOLS FOR CONTINUOUS IMPROVEMENT

Standard Approach and Outcome:

- View risk assessments and audits as compliance checks to be completed and filed away.
- Example: Using risk assessments and audits solely to satisfy regulatory requirements.
- Outcome: Minimal engagement with feedback and limited improvement.

Counterintuitive Approach and Expected Outcome:

- Use risk assessments and audits as feedback loops to continuously improve and adapt, seeing them as opportunities for growth.
- Example: Professional fiduciary firms leverage audits and risk assessments to test changes, refine practices and ensure an enduring solution.
- Expected Outcome: Enhanced adaptive solutions and proactive identification of opportunities to solidify processes.

3. OPTIMAL CONFLICT AND GOOD PROBLEMS AS CATALYSTS FOR GROWTH

Standard Approach and Outcome:

- Avoid problems and conflicts to maintain stability and minimize disruption.
- Example: Steering clear of challenging situations to keep operations smooth and predictable.
- Outcome: Stability and internal safety. Maintain status quo.

Counterintuitive Approach and Expected Outcome:

- Embrace optimal conflict and good problems as catalysts for innovation and personal growth.

- Example: See difficult problems as opportunities to reveal limits and drive adaptive solutions.
- Expected Outcome: Transformative change and expanded capabilities driven by challenging situations.

CHAPTER 9

VANQUISHING THE INVISIBLE THREAT

W HEW, IT'S BEEN A LONG, WILD RIDE TO GET HERE, but we have arrived at the book's final chapter—and the culmination of your adaptive journey toward a whole new way of looking at your fiduciary landscape and ultimately ridding your organization of the Invisible Threat.

Throughout the book, we've been exploring the intricate world of professional fiduciary services as it exists today, a trust industry that resides within the wealth management landscape. We've seen how this broader wealth management industry has evolved into a complex mix of financial institutions, and continues to diversify and expand its products and services to meet the growing needs of its customers in the digital age.

In Chapter 1 we gave you a historical backdrop for understanding how the trust industry got to where it is today, how it has become the norm for professional fiduciary firms to be affiliated with, or provide services on behalf of, companies established under and required to operate within the completely different securities regulatory frameworks.

Through the chapters that followed, we highlighted some unique challenges that come with providing professional trustee services in this combustible environment. Today's wealth management industry is filled with organizational combinations whose businesses are not fully integrated with one another and who inevitably struggle to succeed—each probably inside their own siloed regulatory framework—without fully understanding why they can never quite close the gap between where their organization is and where it wants to be. This gap remains a common problem across the industry.

It is an industry haunted, unknowingly, by what we've called the Invisible Threat: the poorly aligned, diverse services that creates hidden assumptions and obstacles within organizations in today's complex wealth management landscape.

It's not the misalignment of services itself that constitutes the threat; it's our inability to see the misalignment. In other words, the problem is not that this threat to your organization exists at all, but that it remains invisible to you.

Maybe you're thinking to yourself, *Ah that makes sense, no wonder our organization has a gap, but now I've read the book and so the threat has become visible to me.* Well yes, that's a good start, but it does not mean your problem is solved. There's more to vanquishing the Invisible Threat than just absorbing the theoretical understanding of how today's wealth management industry consists of various, and possibly combustible, combinations of diverse businesses. In this book, we have attempted to show how this misalignment constitutes a real and pressing issue, affecting many professional fiduciary firms and wealth management organizations today. But every financial institution is unique, and you need to learn to see and identify the particular way the Invisible Threat manifests in yours.

This is crucial for anyone looking to navigate this industry successfully. It's why you picked up this book. And now you are almost there. In the earlier chapters, we showed you a number of good approaches and strategies to tackle the challenges that you now understand as rooted in the Invisible Threat. We outlined the importance of seeing hidden assumptions, getting the right help, entering new gates (that require a different lens to see), recognizing adaptive challenges, and striving for win-win solutions. We wrote the book in a way that, we hope, allows you to see how each chapter builds on the previous, creating a momentum to ultimately vanquish the Invisible Threat.

Here in Chapter 9, we bring all these pieces together. This final chapter is the peak of your journey. It offers a clear road map to help you vanquish the threat for once and, when you've ensured an enduring solution, hopefully for all. We also revisit some of the most important counterintuitive ideas and key points from across the book and show how they can be combined and applied in practical, effective ways.

Our goal is to leave you with a strong actionable understanding of how to move forward from here. We want to empower you to tackle any invisible threats with confidence and clarity. Now that you've reached this point in the book, you possess a strong knowledge and awareness of the tools you can use to not only identify and understand these hidden challenges, but also overcome them, transforming your organization and making it that much more adaptive and resilient.

So, without further ado, let's jump in and explore how to turn these concepts and strategies into concrete actions that will help you succeed in this ever-evolving landscape of trust and wealth management.

OUR TOP FIVE COUNTERINTUITIVE IDEAS FOR VANQUISHING THE INVISIBLE THREAT

Throughout the book we've introduced several concepts that are explicitly counterintuitive, challenging traditional thinking. At the end of each chapter, we highlighted how these ideas often contradict conventional wisdom, particularly for professional fiduciary firms operating within a larger wealth management organization. Now we want to revisit the five most impactful counterintuitive concepts. These ideas are essential for tackling the Invisible Threat and offering fresh perspectives that can lead to breakthrough solutions:

1. **Adaptive Challenges Fix the Person.** Conventional wisdom tells us that problems can be fixed with the right technical solutions and our existing knowledge. However, adaptive challenges are different—they require us to change ourselves, to shift our mindsets and behaviors. Overcoming the Invisible Threat is not just about fixing our systems; it's about the way we look at problems. Remember, good problems solve us.[29]

GOOD PROBLEMS SOLVE US.

---

2. **Seeing the Hidden Assumptions.** Often, we focus on fixing surface-level issues, but these are usually symptoms of deeper, hidden assumptions. To truly address the Invisible Threat, we must identify and challenge these underlying assumptions. By doing so, we expose the core issues and eliminate obstacles that really matter.

3. **The Importance of Informal Authority.** While formal

authority relies on top-down directives, informal authority—built through relationships and influence—can often be more effective. Leveraging this informal authority helps build momentum for adaptive change. To overcome the Invisible Threat, tapping into these informal networks is key to creating breakthroughs.

4. **Embracing Complexity and Uncertainty.** It's human nature to crave certainty and control, but adaptive challenges are inherently complex and uncertain. Instead of resisting this uncertainty, we must embrace it. To navigate the Invisible Threat, we need to be comfortable with not having all the answers upfront and adapt as circumstances evolve.

5. **Win-Win Solutions through Adaptive Change.** Traditional approaches often focus on compromise in the face of conflicting interests. Adaptive change, however, pushes us to find win-win solutions that maximize benefits for everyone involved. By doing so we foster collaboration and ensure that changes are sustainable. This is key to dismantling the Invisible Threat.

By revisiting these counterintuitive ideas and seeing how they challenge conventional wisdom, we equip ourselves with the tools and mindset needed to recognize and reduce the impact of the Invisible Threat.

WHAT ABOUT LEVERAGE POINTS?

In Chapter 5 we introduced the concept of leveraging informal authority within an organization—working with the people inside your professional fiduciary firm to align everyone with the organization's goals and needs, and to strategically remove invisible threats through collaborative decision-making. Then, in Chapter 6 we demonstrated how you could leverage your unique ability as an informal authority to provoke changes in your environment and remove obstacles to bring about adaptive change. By that point, you too will be more than willing to embrace the adaptive change and start down the adaptive path. But with the myriad of problems facing your organization, the question becomes, once again, how do you even know where to begin?

And to that, we ask the following question of you: what if you were able to provoke change at a crucial leverage point, a specific place where your efforts would be maximized to produce the most significant results?

Sounds reasonable, but what exactly do we mean by leverage point? Put simply, Leverage Points are the pressure points that, when pushed correctly and in the right direction, can transform the entire system. They're crucial because they help us focus our efforts on areas that will yield the biggest benefit, making the daunting task of adaptive change that much more manageable.

Provoking at a crucial leverage point will help you eliminate the Invisible Threat through the repeated success of your adaptive changes, not by targeting problems at random—not like that game of Whack-a-Mole we mentioned in Chapter 1, where you spot problems and knock them down, only to have new ones, or even the same ones, continually pop up.

If we allow that it is through the repeated success of your adaptive changes that you will vanquish the Invisible Threat, it only makes sense that what you should be targeting, first and foremost, is the *quality* of those adaptive changes applied within your organization's systems.

YOU VANQUISH THE INVISIBLE THREAT THROUGH THE REPEATED SUCCESS OF YOUR ADAPTIVE CHANGES.

Leverage points are crucial for adaptive change, which often feels overwhelming because it involves complex systems with many moving parts; by identifying and targeting Leverage Points, we are already helping to simplify this process. These points allow us to make strategic changes that ripple throughout the organization, leading to resolution of longstanding issues. And this approach makes breakthroughs not only more achievable but also more sustainable in the long term.

So, let's turn our attention to some of the most important Leverage Points for you to potentially target. In the same way that we revisited the top five counterintuitive ideas identified on our journey for tackling the Invisible Threat, here are the top five Leverage Points that can help you implement these ideas effectively.

1. Paradigm / Organization, i.e., the power to *see* a paradigm as such; a lens to a new way of seeing
    A. *Why It's a Leverage Point:* Seeing a paradigm for what it is brings awareness of other paradigms. It's a leverage point because people can either refuse to believe what they see or accept the lens to a new way of seeing.
    B. *Reason for Leverage:* Looking through a different lens influences all decisions and actions within the organization. With the right lens, we are able to see the Invisible Threat facing the organization.

2. **Mindset, i.e., the plan out of which the business arises**
   A. *Why It's a Leverage Point:* The foundational assumptions and beliefs of a business—the business plan adopted by people within the organization—determines its overall direction and strategy. We call this mindset, and it's a leverage point because people can either accept those assumptions and beliefs or challenge them.
   B. *Reason for Leverage:* Shifting the mindset allows for challenges to an organization's assumptions and beliefs. With the right mindset, old assumptions and beliefs can be challenged, allowing the organization to vanquish the Invisible Threat.

3. **Rules, i.e., the rules of the organization**
   A. *Why It's a Leverage Point:* The rules of an organization define its scope, constraints, incentives, and punishments, all of which dictate behavior within an organization. It is the organization's formal authority structure that designs and controls those rules. These rules are a leverage point because rules can remain firmly fixed under the sole control of formal authority or allowed to change under the influence of informal authority.
   B. *Reason for Leverage:* By allowing those with only informal authority to provoke change, organizational rules and behaviors can shift. This fosters a more flexible and responsive set of rules, better positioning the organization for adaptive changes needed to vanquish the Invisible Threat.

4. **Structure, i.e., ability to self-organize, or the power to evolve**
   A. *Why It's a Leverage Point:* Changing its business or operational structures allows an organization to adjust to unforeseen circumstances. This ability to self-organize,

or power to evolve, is a leverage point because organizations can choose to implement only known solutions, with expected outcomes, and keep its current structures or accept adaptive solutions, with unknown outcomes, to evolve its structures.

B. *Reason for Leverage:* Adaptive solutions embrace uncertainty and enable self-organization, enhancing the organization's resilience and ability to evolve through successive adaptive challenges from the Invisible Threat.

5. Goals, i.e., the goals of the business

A. *Why It's a Leverage Point:* Goals are what define a business's purpose and direction, influencing all strategic decisions. They are a leverage point because everything else within that organization, even its ability to self-organize, will be influenced by them.

B. *Reason for Leverage:* Aligning goals with desired outcomes that benefit all stakeholders, using adaptive solutions, ensures a win-win focus. This drives the organization towards enduring, sustainable success by making its culture more adaptive and inclusive.

By focusing on these Leverage Points, we can make meaningful progress toward overcoming the Invisible Threat. These points are not just theoretical concepts—they are practical tools that, when applied with adaptive solutions, can lead to profound and lasting change in our organizations.

BRING IT ALL TOGETHER: COMBINE COUNTER-INTUITIVE IDEAS *WITH* LEVERAGE POINTS.

Let's now take a look at how to bring everything together, how these key Leverage Points can be integrated with the key counterintuitive ideas from this chapter to create powerful solutions.

This integration of ideas and Leverage Points won't just solve problems—it will create breakthroughs to new opportunities for growth and resilience. By combining these tools effectively, you will be able to navigate complex challenges and achieve sustainable success.

In fact, people have successfully applied these combinations in all sorts of real-world scenarios to transform their entire lives and, for organizations, their entire business models. In earlier stories, you saw how Matt applied these strategies to his own health and wellness. Now, let's take a look at how exactly he combined counterintuitive ideas and Leverage Points to vanquish his invisible threats.

HOW MATT LEARNED TO TAKE HIS OWN ADVICE

MATT: Before starting Nth Degree, I was working at BMO Bank in Chicago, where I had a great boss named Sohrab Zargham. He was the chief auditor there, and what I loved about working for him was how he gave me and my team so much autonomy. He really let us set our own structure and then supported it. The environment was so collaborative. Under the direct supervision of Doug Duzinskas and Stacey Gohl, I thrived.

By this point in my life, I had already held a number of positions in finance. But with the earlier jobs, for me something had always felt off. It was always the people with formal authority who set policy, made the rules, etc., and I would support whatever path they decided to take. But I didn't like it. It didn't sit well with me. Not because these bosses did anything wrong. I guess I just didn't fit that corporate mold.

With Sohrab, however, the team had the latitude to structure things in whatever way we thought best. It was great. Until one day, it wasn't—at least for me.

"Eby," Sohrab said. "You're a builder. You need to be building." Then, he made it very clear where he was going with all this: "You're wasting your potential." It was time for me to leave. His words hit me like a ton of bricks. It was Mom Florez all over again. But in this case, I didn't need a bunch of brochures. I knew what I had to do. I had already been starting to think about creating my own consulting firm. And deep down, I knew I wasn't going to be working for BMO, or any corporation, for much longer.

Sohrab's comment was the catalyst for my future path. I knew I needed to do something different, something to push myself. Needed to find a different way and a new approach. This was the moment when I began to challenge my own assumptions.

Starting with my assumptions around career, I came to realize that sticking to the traditional corporate ladder wasn't the only way to achieve success. Instead, I began to look differently at the whole idea of professional stability, seeing it as something I could carve out for myself through entrepreneurship and innovation. This shift in mindset represented a critical leverage point—the power to change my own lens or, in other words, shift paradigms. It allowed me to redefine my whole view of career stability and progression.

From there, I began questioning my long-held assumptions about the nature of work itself, which I had always seen as basically a series of tasks established by others. Now, however, I started to view work more as a creative and strategic effort where I could set the agenda and make a direct impact. But this also meant I had to change the rules of my own system, set new standards, and create incentives that aligned with my personal vision for success.

Another area where I had to challenge my assumptions was in my role as leader. I used to think leadership was just about managing staff. But now that I was outside of a traditional corporate structure, I realized I needed to focus on leadership through inspiration. I began to see how I could inspire others to reach beyond their own assumed potential, approach things differently, and push boundaries for themselves, within their organization as well as at the industry level. Challenging my own assumptions about leadership had marked a crucial shift for me, and now I wanted to share my insights across other organizations. And with my new lens, I knew how to make that happen: by driving positive feedback loops that could amplify the impact of leadership.

Finally, I had to challenge my assumptions about success in general. Instead of measuring success with traditional metrics like raises, bonuses, and titles, I realized that it meant something quite different to me. Success became about creating something of lasting value, making a difference, and continuously learning and challenging my own lens.

These were the exciting thoughts that raced through my mind after the initial shock of Sohrab's words. So, I resigned from the bank and created Nth Degree.

I could share more about what this major life change has meant to me, but instead I'm going to turn the rest of this story over to Joanne...

JOANNE: I was working for the same bank when all this was happening with Matt. He had inspired me to move to the US and take the job in Chicago, so I had a front row seat to these events.

While working on the same audit team I got to observe just how good Matt was at seeing through obstacles, cutting through the noise, and using his informal influence to elevate us as a team and as individuals. He had a rare ability to inspire people and empower them to create their own paths.

Which was exactly what he did for himself when he resigned.

Matt took this particular aptitude he had and brought it to his new consulting firm where he seemed certain he could broaden his influence and use the same skillset across a multitude of organizations.

When Matt left BMO to start Nth Degree, it served as a powerful illustration of the concepts we've shared in this book, such as:

1. *Awareness Leading to Adaptive Change:* The story demonstrates that the adaptive challenge fixed the person by showing how Matt, faced with Sohrab's candid feedback, realized he was not reaching his full potential within the corporate structure and brought awareness that the traditional corporate structure was not the only path to success. This prompted him to leave his stable job and start his own consulting firm, Nth Degree. Through this major life change, Matt grew personally and professionally by challenging his beliefs about career stability, leadership, and success. This shift in his lens allowed him to redefine his goals, embrace a new lens, and ultimately become more effective and fulfilled in his work. The challenge pushed Matt to adapt himself and evolve in his career, leading to significant personal and professional development.

2. *Challenging Hidden Assumptions:* The story shows that Matt was able to see and challenge his hidden assumptions, questioning his long-held beliefs about career stability, the nature of work, and leadership. Specifically, he realized that the traditional corporate ladder was not the only path to success and that work could be more than just completing tasks

set by others. He also redefined leadership, from managing staff to inspiring and empowering others. By recognizing and challenging these hidden assumptions, Matt was able to develop new approaches and strategies that aligned better with his personal vision and values.

3. *Building Informal Authority:* The story shows the importance of building informal authority in how Matt used his influence and relationships within the audit team to elevate and inspire his colleagues. Despite not having formal authority, his ability to see through obstacles, cut through noise, and empower his team members demonstrates how informal authority can drive significant positive changes and foster a collaborative and innovative environment. Informal authority—in the form of Sohrab Zargham, Matt's boss—is also what influenced Matt to seek a different career. Sohrab used his influence to provide candid feedback and encouragement. Sohrab's direct and supportive communication, emphasizing Matt's potential and the need for him to pursue something more aligned with his abilities, acted as a catalyst for Matt to leave the corporate job and start his own consulting firm.

4. *Embracing Complexity and Uncertainty:* The story shows the importance of embracing complexity and uncertainty in Matt's decision to leave the stability of his corporate job at BMO Bank and start Nth Degree. This involved navigating the unknowns of entrepreneurship, where he had to adapt to new challenges, create his own systems, and continuously learn and innovate. By embracing this uncertain and complex environment, Matt was able to grow personally and professionally, ultimately finding greater fulfillment and success.

5. *Creating Win-Win Solutions:* The story shows the power of win-win solutions through adaptive change in how Matt and

Nth Degree helped clients create solutions that benefited all stakeholders. By fostering an adaptive culture in his new firm, Matt enabled client organizations to innovate, take ownership of their work, and develop sustainable strategies. This approach ensured that both the clients and their organizations saw positive, lasting impacts, aligning with the principles of win-win solutions. And there was a win-win for Sohrab and BMO as well. By encouraging Matt to pursue his potential outside the Bank, Sohrab helped Matt embark on a fulfilling career path, while also ensuring that the bank's audit team remained aligned with individuals who were fully engaged and satisfied with their roles. Conducting audits had never been Matt's career goal. But working on Sohrab's audit team, alongside Doug and Stacey, allowed Matt to see his Invisible Threat—the threat that was holding him back. Sohrab was the right help for Matt to enter the gate toward his own consulting firm.

What Matt always understood so well was the power of adaptive change, and specifically the importance of mindset and challenging his own lens. He had used that adaptive approach with each audit Sohrab's team worked on, empowering the team to innovate and take ownership of their work and approach to each audit, elevating the reputation of the entire fiduciary audit team.

Matt brought the same adaptive culture to Nth Degree and became increasingly adept as a consultant in helping clients recognize that they too could embrace an adaptive culture, even within a very traditional professional fiduciary firm, could create their own standards, find their own way to cut through the fog, get to the things that make a direct impact for their organization and their own clients, and ensure adaptive solutions were sustainable. Matt himself continued to evolve as a consultant and was able to show clients willing to embrace an adaptive culture that they could, and should, do more than just tweak system parameters; instead, they could actually challenge the very rules of the system.

HOW TO CONTROL A SYSTEM'S PERFORMANCE

Do you want us to reveal the secret to *really* controlling your organization's performance?

Okay, that was a bit of a trick question. There is no magic bullet and by this point the path to success, to vanquishing the Invisible Threat, should not seem like a secret to you. We've been outlining these strategies throughout the book, and our goal now is to bring it all together—counter-intuitive ideas *combined with* Leverage Points. One of the key counterintuitive ideas we've already highlighted is about *seeing* those hidden assumptions that might be holding you back. These are often the very things that entice you to continuously apply the same or similar technical solutions to complex (adaptive) problems. But by changing the lens to see the Invisible Threat and then challenging (invalidating) your assumptions, you can embrace adaptive change to tackle the real issues causing gaps in your system's performance.

You must start by targeting the Leverage Points in your system where small changes can make a big difference. Ask yourself: with all the problems your organization is facing, all the constraints holding it back from success, where in the system is the *one* thing to focus on? What is that *one* leverage point where you can apply a provoke to achieve a meaningful break-through in the system?

Then, once that provoke to the *one* leverage point has

brought about the desired adaptive change, you can ask yourself another question: with all the remaining problems your organization is facing, where in the system is the *next* one thing to focus on?

By focusing on those key Leverage Points—targeting them one after the other as you build on the consecutive successes of your adaptive changes—you can do more than just tweak things a little. You can actually change the rules and take control of the whole system's performance, ultimately vanquishing the Invisible Threat in your organization.

YOU CAN DO MORE THAN JUST TWEAK SYSTEM PARAMETERS; YOU CAN CONTROL PERFORMANCE OF THE ENTIRE SYSTEM.

Before we move on, let's take the opportunity to dig deeper into the concept of Leverage Points. It is not a new concept but one that gained traction in the late nineties with work being done in the field of systems analysis. A well-known pioneering systems analyst at that time, Donella Meadows, explained in one of her best-known essays that Leverage Points are places within a complex system, such as an organization in today's wealth management industry like your professional fiduciary firm, where a small shift in one thing can produce big changes in everything.[30]

Wow, you might be thinking, *that seems too good to be true.* Meadows did indeed concede in her essay that folks who work in systems analysis have a great belief in Leverage Points. But for those of us toiling in the financial services industry, often we have no idea where to even spot the Leverage Points in our organizations. Or at least that's how it feels to many. And if we can't see them, how can we possibly identify the right ones, especially the *one* where we should apply that first provoke?

Meadows goes deep on Leverage Points in her essay, beyond even their use in systems analysis. She points out that the very concept is "embedded in legend" and that we see this in such enduring expressions as "silver bullets," "miracle cures," and "magic passwords."[31] Moreover, we know, all of us, simply from the experience of being human, how seductive it can be to fantasize about a simple, magical solution that would solve all our problems in one fell swoop—if only we could just push the right button. Life is not like that, of course. But the longing says something in itself. In short, we want to believe Leverage Points exist, and want to know where they are so we can get our hands on them. We intuitively understand that "leverage points are points of power."[32] And who among us doesn't want access to that power, especially when it comes to all the daily challenges in our work lives? But when we try to locate those Leverage Points, we still find ourselves at a loss.

The truth, as Meadows reveals in her essay, is that we do in fact have some intuitive sense of where Leverage Points are. Yes, even the Leverage Points in your own complex organization. To illustrate this fact, Meadows quotes in her essay the story that Jay Forrester—a renowned computer engineer, management theorist, and systems scientist at MIT—would often tell about how he went about analyzing a company, looking for and indeed ultimately locating its Leverage Points.[33]

Forrester's success in finding these Leverage Points seems like good news, right? At least it means your organization must already possess such Leverage Points too, and those are the places to focus on. Maybe all you need is the right lens to *see* them, and all will be well. Right?

Not so fast. Yes, your organization has these Leverage Points. And yes, you'll need to see them in order to know where to start. But it's one thing to know intuitively where those Leverage Points are, and quite another to make the adaptive changes necessary to actually close the gap. Once you see a Leverage Point—that *one* point to focus on first—you shouldn't fool yourself into thinking you've found a single magic button. As Meadows pointed out, there are no miracle cures. The reason can be found in the rest of the story that Forrester liked to tell. He would explain that after all of his analysis, which finally led him to that *one* Leverage Point, he would go back to the struggling company only to discover that they had actually already been paying a lot of attention to the very same Leverage Point. Why wasn't it working? If the people in the organization already instinctively knew where the Leverage Point was, what was the problem? Forrester goes on to explain that they were pushing that Leverage Point *in the wrong direction!*[34]

Counterintuitive is the word Forrester used to describe complex systems, such as your professional fiduciary firm in today's broader wealth management landscape. So it's possible, according to Meadows, that even when you know what the *one* Leverage Point is where you should focus on first, your organization is in fact already focusing its efforts there—but has been intuitively pushing at it in the wrong direction, systematically making the problems they are trying to solve even worse.[35]

Now we're getting to the crux of the issue. Here is where we hope this chapter will really start to bring everything together for you: by helping you understand what it means to push a Leverage Point *in the right direction*. Throughout this book we've given you counterintuitive ideas, highlighting five of the most important at the start of this chapter. And we've shown how combining those counterintuitive ideas and Leverage Points can be integrated to create powerful solutions. What follows now is a story about exactly that. In fact, it's a return to the story we told in Chapter 1, the fable of George, a manager for a brokerage firm that acquired a trust company, who was then promoted to head up that new company. The story covered his struggles over those first two years: staffing was a problem, he'd been hammered by the Board because revenue and profits continued to drop, and when we left him, he'd just found out that folks on the brokerage side weren't even promoting the trust company's services!

When we last saw George in Chapter 1, he was also feeling like he could still turn the tide, despite the accumulation of problems he faced. He had told himself that if anyone had what it took to turn the ship around and succeed, it was him, no matter how bad things seemed at the time.

We asked you at the end of that chapter to think about how the story would turn out for George, reminding you that while he was determined, it was obvious his energies were misplaced. You likely sensed George would fail: he was focusing his energies on the wrong things, trying to solve problems while failing to see the underlying issues, the blind spots caused by his hidden assumptions. What George didn't realize—his Invisible Threat— was that he was operating in a fog. And unless that fog cleared, while George might succeed at fixing one or two problems through sheer dint of effort, he would never make the trust company a success story.

Before we dive into the rest of his story, let's take a step back and review some of George's initial assumptions and the problems those assumptions brought to the trust company.

ASSUMPTION #1: TRUST OFFICERS SHOULD DO AS THEY'RE TOLD!

George assumed that trust officers should not question or complain about differences between the way they *used to* do things and the way George wanted them to do things. This assumption was harmful because it undermined the trust officers' professional judgment and expertise. But it also led to bigger problems: when a trust company fails to leverage the knowledge and expertise of its skilled trust officers, asking them instead to just follow orders, it hinders the company's ability to ensure compliance and provide high-quality service to clients.

ASSUMPTION #2: HIGHER FEES WILL IMPROVE THE BOTTOM LINE

George assumed that if the company increased its fees for trust accounts, this would boost revenue and improve the bottom line. But this assumption didn't factor in the loss of existing and prospective business as a result of the higher fees. What actually happened was the fee increase resulted in a *loss* of revenue, not offset by improved services. Because of this, existing clients who had come as part of the initial acquisition started to look for replacement trustees. Then, when the company reversed its approach and offered lower fees to the departing clients, George learned that fees were the least of the problems and the clients had been dissatisfied all along with trustee services post-acquisition. Worse, the brokers in the brokerage division had been advising prospective trust business clients to steer clear of their own trust company!

ASSUMPTION #3: THE CLIENT IN A TRUST BUSINESS IS THE SAME AS THE CLIENT IN A BROKERAGE BUSINESS

George assumed that trust accounts and brokerage accounts could be serviced in the same way. They can't, and this assumption turned out to be harmful because it resulted in inadequate handling of trust-specific requirements, such as income and principal separation, compliance with trust laws, and customized reporting for beneficiaries. Then, with the trust company unable to effectively meet the unique needs of its trust accounts, other problems emerged, including compliance issues and all sorts of general confusion and dissatisfaction. Ultimately, this meant lost clients and reduced revenue.

Given all of these hidden assumptions that George could not see, and the problems they brought to the trust company, what do you think he should do now? Where do you think George should begin? Do you believe he has what it takes to succeed on his own?

The truth is that without the right lens, George will never be able to lift the fog, and will eventually fail, along with the trust company.

We have seen this happen before and there is no doubt it continues to happen to other organizations. The issue is not a lack of will or desire to succeed on George's part. He has worked hard and tried a lot of things over the past two years, without success. But now, if he digs in harder to focus on the bottom line, what might happen to the few remaining skilled trust professionals he has working for him? How can the trust company hang onto its clients when not only are fees being increased but service levels continue to fall off?

Can you spot the Invisible Threat lurking in the fog—the one thing underlying all of George's assumptions and causing the problems?

George cannot see it. It's not the threat itself that's the problem. The problem is that until George has the right lens to *see* the Invisible Threat—to make the invisible visible—no amount of effort or determination can close the gap for George and his trust company. George has a major blind spot and cannot see his current reality for what it actually is. As we noted at the end of Chapter 1, you can't close the gap without first seeing your own hidden assumptions. We also pointed out that it's not such an easy thing to do on your own; you need some expert guidance. So, let's pick up where we left off to see how this might turn out for George—if he's able to get the right help.

FROM BLIND SPOTS TO BRIGHT SPOTS: THE JOURNEY THROUGH ADAPTIVE CHANGE

George had just finished giving himself a pep talk—telling himself that if anyone could turn the tide for the trust company, it was him, no matter how bad things might seem at the moment—when he heard a disruptive banging on his office door. "Door's open," he said, his standard line when he really just wished the staff would stop bothering him with their complaints and bellyaching.

It was the senior trust officer and she looked alarmed. "They're leaving," she said, "better get out here quick!" Then she darted away. Confused, George followed her, only to be almost bowled over when what looked like half of the trust company staff entered his office, each one leaving a piece of paper on his desk. "What's this?" he asked. "What's going on?" As they headed down the hall toward the elevator bank, one of the departing staff half-turned and said, "We quit—we all quit."

George had no words. He moved to his desk and slumped down in his chair. His senior trust officer hovered near the door, but made no move to come in. George finally looked up and asked if she was leaving too. She shook her head no, though it was clear to George she was not only shocked but very unhappy about this turn of events. She gave him a strained look, then straightened up and told him she had a lot of work to do since she was "the last trust officer standing."

George hung his head down. Just moments ago, he'd been so pumped, giving himself a pep talk, telling himself he had this, he'd fix all the problems. But now, it was a different story. He knew beyond a shadow of a doubt that without enough staff it was just a matter of time before the company would cease to operate. He'd failed. Failed as president of the trust company, failed as a leader, and failed at giving his bosses what they'd asked of him. He glanced down at the half-dozen resignation letters on his desk and shuffled through them, wondering if he should type out one for himself.

But he couldn't shake the image of his senior trust officer, standing at his door, in shock and pain, yet somehow managing to dig deep and carry on. Out of all the people who he knew he'd let down in his past, he realized he would never forget her expression. It was a cry for help, but George, finally starting to gain some clarity, knew it was not within him to help her—or the company. He shoved the resignation letters off the top of his desk into a drawer and dropped his face into his hands. There was nothing he could say or do for her; he had no answers.

A short time later, head still in his hands, he heard his door close quietly and looked up, expecting to see his boss with a pink slip. Instead, feeling like he was dreaming, he saw the company lawyer he'd been thinking about earlier that morning—someone he had barely ever seen in the building over the past two years—and now here he was sitting in George's visitor chair.

"Name's Bob," the lawyer reminded George, and stuck out

his hand. George reached out a weak arm only to feel his hand gripped in a firm handshake. "Heard things might be rough going for you right about now. My offer still stands—if you want some advice on the trust business."

George merely shook his head numbly. "It's too late," he said, "it's all over. I'll just let the Board know we need to close down the business."

"Well," Bob said, "that's an interesting thought. But not as easy as you might think, my fellow. You see, you're managing a trust company. And your trust company has signed a lot of trust agreements. Written agreements where you agreed to accept appointment as trustee of a lot of trusts. Those are not simple legal contracts where you can just quit." George heard the words, but they made no sense. This was another new and strange thing—they couldn't quit the business?

"What're we supposed to do?" George asked. "We can't operate without staff and half of them just walked out the door."

"Come with me," Bob said, and led the way to the senior trust officer's office. Her door was open, but Bob stopped well beyond it—close enough to look in without interrupting her as she talked on the phone while typing on her computer. "Sandy's still here," he said. "She knows the company has a duty as trustee of the trusts and she's trying her best to get through this tough time. She also assumes you know the trust company has a duty and is expecting you to lead the rest of the staff through this challenge."

"What are you talking about?" George asked. "What duty? Half the staff quit—they didn't seem to think they owed me a duty."

"Well, those people were your recent trust officer hires—and they were all new to the trust industry. They didn't think they owed anyone any duty, particularly not to the trusts, and cer-

tainly not to you. Let's go to my office so we don't disturb Sandy."
George meekly followed Bob to his office.

A few hours later, George, still in Bob's office, put up both his hands and said, "Enough. I can't absorb anything else. I'm still not sure I understand even half of what you've been telling me, except for one thing. And that one thing—which makes me feel mighty stupid to admit, but I feel I can trust you enough to say this—is I've been running this trust company all wrong. I've been running it the only way I knew, and I know only how to manage a brokerage team. I don't know why I never saw that before. I assumed since my brokerage firm bought the trust company, it was ours to run the way it suited us. We wanted a trust company to bring in more brokerage business—now you're telling me that's all wrong?"

Bob nodded in agreement.

George said, "Well, there's even less reason for me to stay on then. I don't know what I'm doing. I should hand in my notice and follow those people out."

"Yes," Bob said, "that's what you could do on the brokerage side. But think of Sandy. She is frightened, but she's experienced enough in the trust business to understand the trust company can't just shut its doors. There are beneficiaries of trusts expecting disbursements—they depend on those funds to live. There are parents of special needs beneficiaries—they depend on this trust company to be around to help their special needs children when they're no longer around. There are grantors of gifting trusts, expecting you to accept contributions, mail out withdrawal notices, and invest the assets wisely to benefit not only their next generation, but the generations after that. I could go on, but I can see you are exhausted."

"So," George responded, "if you know so much about this, why'd you wait until I was at the very end of my rope before stopping by to offer me some help?"

"I offered to help you two years ago," Bob said, "and you could have found my office. Why didn't you?"

"Well," George said, "I guess I didn't think I needed the help. I knew what I was doing. Or at least, if it had been a brokerage team, I think I would have been doing the right things." Then, grudgingly, George admitted that even if Bob had stopped by to offer some unsolicited advice, George would have thought he was nagging him and would have ignored all that Bob tried to tell him.

"So," George finally asked, "what do I do next?"

"I can't tell you that," Bob answered. "You have a lot of work ahead of you if you still want to make a go of things. But with or without you, the trust company will have to at least limp along until it can be sold, or folded into another, stronger, trust company to take on the administration of the trusts. So why not think things through and stop by in the morning. You might have more questions and I'd be happy to answer them."

That night George barely slept. He felt like an idiot. Bob had told him all about what he called "big-F Fiduciary" and the fiduciary duties the trust company had under the regulations, as well as under what Bob referred to as common law. He also mentioned "applicable laws," mirroring what his senior trust officer (who, with Bob's help, he realized he should probably start calling by name, Sandy, instead of his usual "hey, you") had been trying to tell him about for at least a year or more.

When he got to the office the next morning, his first stop was Sandy's office. "Good morning, Sandy," he said. "And thank you for hanging in there with me." She merely glanced up at him, already engrossed in her work and looking, if anything, more exhausted than George felt.

His second stop was Bob's office and this time he went in and sat down. "Okay," he said, "thank you for your help yesterday. I can't say I really understand everything, or anything, about the trust company business, but I'm in. I realize I have to let go of what I thought I knew and embrace whatever the path ahead brings me. So, tell me, am I crazy to think I have even a chance to succeed?"

Bob leaned over his desk and looked right into George's eyes, like he was searching for something. Then he sat back and smiled as he answered, "Yes, in some way you are crazy, because the path you're choosing is hard. You can't even see, never mind imagine, all the obstacles in the way. The path is a hard one because you have to adapt. You have to fix you. But I can see it in your eyes—you've accepted the help I offered and, despite not knowing what lies ahead, you are determined to take the hard path to adaptive change. And you might think me crazy too, but, somehow, I believe you have a chance to succeed."

George tried to give a little grin, but sensed it came out more like a grimace, then said, "I feel like I've been talking to some guru. But you've managed to get through to my thick skull, so as long as you're willing to coach me along from time to time, I'm willing to change."

George headed back to Sandy's office and this time, rather than barging in, he respectfully tapped on her open door. She glanced up, looking distracted and distraught. "What?" she asked. "Can't you see I'm busy? I'm the only trust officer left and I need to approve a lot of cash disbursements this morning."

"Yes," George answered, "I know you're busy, Sandy. I just wanted to know if I can take you to lunch today—we need to talk."

Sandy just shook her head, saying, "You still don't get it. I'm the *only* trust officer left. What on earth makes you think I even have time to go out for lunch?"

"I'm sorry," George said, uncharacteristically patient.

That seemed to get Sandy's attention for a moment. She put down the papers she'd been reviewing and sighed, saying, "Look, I brought my lunch, I'm fine, but if you want to talk, I can stop by your office at one o'clock."

To that, George responded, "One o'clock is fine, and I'll come to your office for a change."

George couldn't settle down to anything the rest of the morning. He opened his desk drawer to go through the resignation letters once more, before sending an email to HR to let them know about the employee termination paperwork they'd need to do. He pecked at a few more emails, then just sat, staring into space until it was time to go to Sandy's office. He felt as nervous as a schoolkid having to go to the principal's office to explain his bad behavior. And no wonder, he thought, remembering all those times he'd ignored or brushed away things Sandy had tried to tell him. Now it was time for him to face facts, and who better to explain those facts to him, he thought, than Sandy.

As soon as he took a seat in her office, Sandy made no bones about telling him right off the bat that he'd never listened to her before, had ignored her every effort to explain why things had to be done differently in the trust company than on the brokerage side. She said she'd asked Bob to talk with him yesterday, something George hadn't realized, but Sandy also said she doubted very much that a few hours with Bob could have magically changed George's true colors. She told George he was a dyed-in-the-wool broker at heart and would never be able to successfully run the trust company. The best thing George could do, she continued, would be to go back to the brokerage side and leave her alone.

George let her talk. In all his years of management, he'd never even imagined allowing a staff person to talk to him like that. But he could see Sandy was feeling a lot of pain and sensed her need to vent. So, for once he just listened. After she'd let off steam for ten minutes or so, she finally got down to brass tacks. "I need two good hires as quickly as possible," said Sandy. "Here are their resumes. They are both skilled trust officers and will be of great help around here. And I'll take it on faith that after your conversation with Bob you'll at least be able to let us *do our jobs*, but this time, the *right* way." She handed George two resumes and turned back to her computer.

Less than fifteen minutes after his meeting with Sandy had started, he was back in his office, feeling quite chagrined and not a whole lot wiser. But Sandy had given him his marching orders. He looked closely at each of the resumes. The names seemed familiar. He checked his staffing folder and looked through copies of resumes he'd received since heading up the trust company, resumes of those he'd hired and those he'd just passed over. And there they both were, the same two people Sandy wanted him to hire, who he hadn't even bothered to interview. And why would he have? They each worked for a bank—different local banks in the area—and had absolutely no brokerage experience on their resumes. He'd known at the time that he needed to hire for the trust company, but he also thought he should stick with people who at least had some brokerage experience. After all, the trust company had been acquired by his brokerage firm, so it made sense to him at the time that new hires should at least understand the brokerage side of the business.

George took a deep breath, feeling the tug of old habits, his comfort with hiring people who spoke the same brokerage language he understood, and his discomfort with hiring people whose skills and job experience were completely foreign to him. He started rifling through some other resumes he had, particularly those that had come to him from internal people already working on the brokerage side. They would be great hires and he could get them to start immediately, which would help Sandy even more! Then George recalled the words he'd spoken to Bob that very morning: "I have to let go of what I thought I knew and embrace whatever the path ahead brings me." Without further ado, he turned to the phone and called the number on one of the resumes Sandy had given him. *After all*, he thought as the phone at the other end started to ring, *I'm president of a trust company so maybe I'd better start behaving like one.*

Much to George's surprise, when he called the two people Sandy recommended, they were both more than willing. He'd feared Sandy had complained to them about how terrible it was to work for him and they'd refuse to even go through an interview. Yet both had accepted the job and showed up two weeks later, ready to start. And start they had! By the end of their first week alone, Sandy looked noticeably calmer.

After their second week, Sandy stopped by George's office to let him know she would be setting up a weekly meeting to discuss matters involving the trust accounts and asked if he would be okay if they held the meeting in his office. For the briefest of moments, George thought she was asking to just literally *use* his office, since it was the biggest one in the trust company, and was about to meekly agree—thinking he could just skip out to lunch while they met. But then he realized she meant him being part of the meeting too. He caught her eye and saw something he'd never seen from her before; he realized it was a ray of hope. Feeling overcome and not wanting her to hear a tremble in his voice, he merely nodded and smiled.

When the meeting invite came through, he accepted it immediately. He had no idea what the meeting was going to entail, but in the month since he'd first spoken with Bob, he'd adapted his approach with Sandy. It was hard at first. As busy as she was, she would just walk by and bark out what seemed like orders, or send curt emails asking his permission for things he didn't understand. She'd always been a bit bossy like that, and George used to fight her on almost everything. She always seemed to want to do things her way, rather than the way George thought things should go. In thinking back, George remembered some of the arguments they'd had, like the one about the trust system she wanted, instead of the brokerage platform George knew his bosses thought they should use to save money, or the whole dual cash thing, which he still wasn't quite clear on.

What kept George going that first month were the words he distinctly remembered Bob telling him, the words he spoke when he realized George was ready to change. He'd told George the path he was choosing was a hard one because he would have to change himself. Bob had seemed convinced George was determined to take the hard path to adaptive change, but on the inside the truth was George just felt afraid. Afraid he'd already failed. Afraid he couldn't recover. And afraid to admit to his failure. He was also afraid to admit to Sandy that he'd been wrong all along. George had never experienced that kind of not-knowing in his career before, so he believed it all the more when Bob told him that day, "You have to fix you."

It was with an open mind that George accepted Sandy's requests and demands that first month without question. He didn't feel like she was trying to boss him around in a harmful way, so he wasn't offended. He sensed Sandy was trying to solve what seemed like a lot of problems—things he couldn't fully grasp—but hoped that solving them would help the trust company. At first, he'd agree and try to get her what she needed without question. Then, after the two new trust officers started, he would occasionally ask Sandy for more information, trying to understand why something was a problem or why she thought something he could do would help solve it. And Sandy started to take the time, once again, to explain things. The difference this time around, however, was George had adapted. He listened, rather than argued, and when he didn't understand something, Sandy didn't seem the least bit annoyed and took the time to help him understand.

During that first weekly meeting in his office, George barely uttered a word. But listen he did. He felt like an interloper, as though he were sitting at an outdoor café in a foreign country eavesdropping on the conversation at the next table, even though he couldn't understand a single word. He remembered the feeling he had during the third weekly meeting, when all three trust officers turned to him and asked if he could find it in the budget to hire a few trust associates—they had just the people for him to hire. George felt thrilled there was something he could finally do to be useful. He asked them why they didn't need three more trust officers instead. After all, six of them had walked out the door. And he grew thoughtful after they explained they needed the *right* help now, that the three of them had the trust officer expertise sufficient for the company's current book of business but the addition of junior associates to assist them would position the team for future growth while keeping salary expenses reasonable.

Six months later, George found himself sitting in his office wrapping up another weekly meeting with his trio of trust officers. He no longer felt like an interloper. Though it had only been six months, he had changed. And learned. Slowly at first, stumbling through terminology he thought meant one thing, which it did on the brokerage side, only to learn it meant something else entirely on the trust company side. And he liked the dynamic of the trio of trust officers. Sandy had never been a good fit with the people he'd previously hired, the ones he'd hired for their brokerage knowledge. But now he recognized that while they might have been decent hires for one of the broker divisions he used to manage, they didn't know enough to work in the trust company and Sandy didn't have the time to teach them while trying to manage a full workload herself. Before they all quit that day, with barely a backward glance, the problems had been piling up, there were numerous complaints, they kept losing clients, and the bottom line was looking further and further away.

At the end of that weekly meeting with his trust officers, it was with a genuine grin on George's face that he shared some good news. Over the past month, they had lost only one account, while accepting three new ones, and the compliance officer had stopped by earlier to let him know that no complaints (zero!) had come in during the last month. George expected high-fives all round, so was surprised by their sudden silence. Sandy finally asked if he had to report the company's numbers to the Board soon? George nodded and Sandy said, "We have a lot of catching up to do—we lost quite a bit of business this past year. Don't you think we should be trying to bring on more accounts? Only three accounts this month is a small number. It seems like we have fewer new account prospects every month."

George thought for a moment, then nodded his agreement, saying, "You know what, now that I think about it, you're right. Maybe our salesperson has been holding off, knowing how busy you guys are."

"Well," said Sandy, "we've been working hard and have things under control now. We still have more work to do, but we know we should be bringing on more new accounts or we won't make our bottom line. We've been meeting with the operations team and have streamlined a lot of our processes so we'll be able to handle the extra workload."

"Wait a minute," George asked, "you've been meeting with operations? I thought you hated them?"

Sandy laughed. "I don't 'hate' them," she said, "I thought their processes were outdated and cumbersome and they didn't know enough about the trust business to understand what we needed."

"What changed?" George asked.

Sandy explained that with the new trust associate hires, she and the other two trust officers had time to meet with the operations people. At first, it was just to educate them, so they could understand why certain things were really important, like timely disbursements to beneficiaries and accurate set up of accounts. But then the operations staff had gotten excited. They had new ideas they thought might help the trust officers, especially after all those other people had just up and quit. So, the two groups—administration and operations—began getting together regularly to solve problems and came up with some innovative solutions that saved time in the short term and would allow them to bring on new accounts quickly and improve the bottom line.

"Wow," George said, "you've been busy. But how did you find out about my bottom line problems—all of that is confidential."

Sandy laughed again, something George had never heard from her until he'd begun to change, to *fix himself* as he liked to think of it, and he liked the sound of that laughter. It was just common sense, Sandy explained: "When we were losing more accounts than we were bringing in, especially those larger accounts, we lost those fees. And we've been around long enough to know examiners look closely at our earnings. They expect a trust company to be reasonably compensated so it can remain in business."

"Really?" George asked. "Our examiner checks *that* out— why?" Sandy reminded George that as a trust company, they had undertaken certain duties and were expected to earn enough to remain in business in order to meet those duties. George nodded, realizing he liked to learn these new tidbits about the trust company. Though he'd been heading up the trust company for two and a half years, only now was he starting to *believe* he might grow into the role as he continued on his adaptive journey.

George's meeting the next day with Fred, the trust company's salesperson, did not go at all the way he expected. Like his meeting with Sandy not so very long ago, it lasted less than fifteen minutes. He'd invited Fred to his office so he could explain that Fred could begin to turn on the tap again and bring on new trust accounts. But after he explained it, Fred looked dumbfounded. "What do you mean, 'turn on the tap again'?" Fred asked. "What makes you think I turned it off? I'm bringing in more business than we can handle."

George showed Fred the numbers, saying, "Look here, just three new ones last month, five the month before, but then just two the month before that, and we had a few months with no new accounts at all."

Fred shook his head at George. "You've got it all wrong," he said, "you're only looking at the trust accounts you opened in the trust company. I've brought in at least a couple hundred new trusts this year alone—I'm averaging nearly fifty new accounts a month!"

After some back and forth, something finally dawned on George. "Wait a minute. You're selling brokerage services to trusts. Is that what you're telling me?"

"Of course," Fred said, "that's what I've been trying to tell you. I'm busier than I've ever been when I used to sell retail brokerage accounts to individuals. I used to have to explain to people what a brokerage account was and why they would need one. But since you brought me on as a salesperson for the trust company, I'm meeting all kinds of people who have trusts that need the brokerage advisory services we sell. Business is booming." Fred sat back and beamed at George.

George hung down his head. He didn't have the heart to tell Fred to his face that he was selling *the wrong thing*. Fred needed to sell the company's trust services; that's the only way the trust company would survive. Instead, Fred was selling brokerage services to trusts that didn't need, or maybe didn't even know about, the trust company's administrative services. The brokerage side was doing well with all that new business, but it made no sense for them to have acquired a trust company and not sell the trust services it could provide. George explained to Fred that he'd been doing great, so great that George would speak to his old boss and get Fred back working directly on the brokerage side again. Fred looked ecstatic at this news. "But who will be your salesperson?" he asked George.

"Look," George said, "just make sure I get your newest, greenest salesperson from the brokerage side. The less they know about the brokerage business the better."

"Really?" Fred asked. "I know they just got a new guy, name's Vinnie. We *had* to hire him. His Dad's an old college buddy of our sales manager. He knows nothing about anything. You want him?"

"Yes," George replied. And with that, Fred was gone. The next day a kid showed up, smiling from ear to ear, dressed in a suit and tie that looked like something he might have borrowed from his father, with a briefcase that looked like it could have belonged to his grandfather. George liked him immediately. "Have a seat, kid," he said, "and take out that pad of paper and pen I know you have in your briefcase." Vinnie did as he was told, then looked up expectantly. George nodded and told him to buckle his seatbelt, he was in for the ride of his life. With that, Vinnie's new career path as the trust company's salesperson took off.

A year later, George could not be more pleased with the upward trajectory the trust company had taken. Sales had exploded once Vinnie finished learning all about the trust business from Sandy and the rest of the administration and operations teams. George agreed to negotiate trust fees, bringing them back into the more competitive range they'd been before he'd increased them; and not only did they get the new business, they retained it. The Board was finally satisfied with the improvement to the bottom line, but let George know they expected continued growth and profitability.

George had also introduced an idea at one of his weekly meetings—now attended by representatives from both the administration and operations teams, along with the ever-smiling Vinnie. Initially, he had been afraid to mention it, but then saw, with his newfound clarity, that it was okay now. He'd earned the trust of the team. So he introduced his idea of inviting over brokers who handled client relationships for the trust company's trusts to spend time in the trust company. He thought they could call it "Shadow Sandy for a Day." The team loved the idea. They agreed it would help the brokers understand the trust business better, which could only help reduce confusion and hopefully enhance client satisfaction.

At first, there was some resistance from the brokerage side, even though the initiative was purely voluntary. It was Vinnie who finally convinced a broker for a brand new trust account to spend a day with Sandy. And the initiative took off from there. Each time a broker had this experience and went back to the brokerage side, they would talk about how different the trust company was from what they thought it was. Soon George's inbox was flooded with emails from brokers wanting to sit with Sandy. But they all realized she still needed to be able to do her work and having a new person sit with her every day was just not viable.

So the team put their heads together and came up with the novel idea of seconding someone from the brokerage side for three months, like a type of internship, and having them work with and for the trust company, learning all they could during that time. The team developed a training plan that included working directly with selected trust company personnel along with educational activities. Three months, they felt, was enough to get a sense of what the trust company actually did. And they could only take on one person at a time. As excited as they were about the plan, they were afraid no one would be willing to do it, or see it for the opportunity it was. Thankfully, their fears were unfounded. It proved to be a popular program indeed. What's more, over time, the trust company even decided to keep on someone who had signed up for the three months and wanted to extend their time with the trust company, to stay on for a maximum of two years. Actually, it was two years minus one day so they wouldn't lose their broker credentials.

Not surprisingly, over the years a few other interns from the brokerage side even elected to stay on with the trust company permanently, willingly giving up those credentials.

Flash forward to ten years later, and George was sitting in his office reminiscing about just how much he'd changed during this fateful period a decade earlier. His memories of that first day he'd talked with Bob were fresh in his mind, due in no small part to the joyous retirement party they'd had for Bob the day before. George knew he'd miss the opportunity to stop by Bob's office to ask random questions, but in reflecting back he also understood that Bob didn't force him to change. George had to get to that point himself. And he was proud he hadn't just given up and quit. He'd learned so much, and continued to learn things about the trust industry practically on a daily basis. He'd also accomplished a lot and remembered the day he'd been able to present a satisfactory audit report to the Board. They didn't know the details of all of the work that had been done to get there, but they recognized the report as a win for the trust company. Since then, George had regained their full confidence and they continued to support him. Even the exams had improved over time, and George was pleased when he'd learned from the compliance officer that their risk had been lowered to allow for less frequent examinations—a win-win solution for both their trust company and the busy state examiners.

All things considered, George was happier now than he would have ever thought possible on that terrible day when he got the stack of resignations. While there were still plenty of bad days at the office, there were far more good days. George reflected humbly on how, when all the old trust officers quit and things were looking so bleak, Sandy had saved him by asking Bob to help him. Life was so different now. Above all, George and his team thrived in their new environment. The adaptive culture they'd built continued to provide them with adaptive challenges, opportunities to continually learn and improve as their journey progressed ever onward.

GEORGE HAS THE RIGHT STUFF

In Chapter 1 we noted that in his zeal to fix all the problems in front of him, George had a dangerous blind spot. This was his Invisible Threat. But because George didn't have the right lens, he couldn't *see* it. Not until he got the right help, that is. And securing the right lens was only the start. You see, George had been pushed to the edge of his knowledge—he knew only how to manage a brokerage team. In other words, he had reached the point of optimal conflict.

We introduced the concept of optimal conflict in Chapter

6. It is a state of being that fosters growth and innovation by pushing teams to the edge of their comfort zones, serving as the catalyst and inspiration for resolution and innovative breakthrough. When all those people quit that day, it raised the heat on issues in the trust company—not only for George, but for Sandy and the others left behind. As we noted in Chapter 6, in the face of adaptive challenges where problems and solutions are unknown, collaborative decision-making becomes essential.

Consider what happened in the story. George was in a dilemma. He wanted to just walk away, but that look in Sandy's eyes when she realized she was the last trust officer standing touched something in him. He wanted to help her. But he was also himself in an optimal conflict because he'd reached the edge of his knowledge. When Sandy, who had only informal authority, began to direct his next steps by giving him those resumes, George began his adaptive change by collaborating, instead of arguing, with her. Once the other trust officers came on board, not only did the administrative group collaborate with one another and with George, they also collaborated with the operations area. And while adaptive change in the trust company didn't begin until George, and those remaining, reached the point of optimal conflict, before long it became the standard approach, allowing the entire trust company to first stabilize, and then thrive, within a relatively short time frame.

We pointed out in Chapter 1 that the George story was an amalgam of client issues we'd come across through our years in the business. The same holds true for this second half of George's story, where we continue to incorporate an amalgam of things we've come across in the past—this time more good things than bad—so the details of his story will, we trust, continue to prove relevant and instructive. And just in case you're wondering, yes, at one firm we worked with, all the trust officers but one did quit all at once, leaving just that one standing.

George's story is written to demonstrate the potential of adaptive change and the remarkable impact it can have when we are willing to confront our own blind spots, challenge underlying assumptions, and embrace the unknown. At the beginning of his journey, George was confident in his ability to turn things around, yet his misplaced energies and blind spots were the very barriers to his success. Here are some of the ways he eliminated those barriers:

CONFRONTING BLIND SPOTS AND CHANGING HIS LENS

At the outset, George's approach was marked by rigid thinking and an inability to see the deeper issues plaguing the trust company. His initial attempts to impose brokerage standards on trust requirements only made things worse. When the majority of his staff resigned, George was placed into optimal conflict with no choice but to face the reality that he had no answer.

In that moment of shock, George finally recognized his major blind spot: his lack of understanding of the trust industry's unique needs. It was this epiphany, coupled with the support of Bob, the company lawyer, that cleared the fog, allowing him to see the Invisible Threat—to shed his blinds spots and finally accept what he was seeing—that sparked his journey. George learned that to solve the company's problems, he needed to first fix himself, by changing his lens and adopting a mindset open to adaptive change.

CHALLENGING UNDERLYING ASSUMPTIONS

George's journey through adaptive change was deeply rooted in challenging his underlying assumptions. Initially, he believed that trust officers should simply follow his directives without question, that hiring trust officers experienced in the brokerage industry would solve staffing issues, and that increasing fees would directly improve the bottom line.

Through his conversations with Bob and Sandy, George began to see the flaws in these assumptions. He realized that respecting the expertise of trust officers, understanding the specific skills needed for trust administration, and considering the broader implications of fee changes were crucial steps in addressing the core issues. By questioning and challenging these assumptions, George paved the way for more effective and informed decision-making.

GETTING THE RIGHT HELP

One of the main breakthroughs in George's story was his willingness to seek and accept the right help. Bob's offer to assist George was initially ignored, but as the gravity of the situation sank in, George understood the value of external perspective and expertise. Bob's guidance on fiduciary duties and the operational realities of the trust business provided George with a much-needed provoke to navigate the complexities he faced.

Sandy's input was also instrumental. Her deep understanding of a trustee's duty and her candid feedback were invaluable, and by relying on Sandy's expertise and following her guidance, George began to make better, faster decisions.

BUILDING INFORMAL AUTHORITY

A significant aspect of George's adaptive change involved leveraging informal authority. Initially, George relied heavily on his own formal authority, expecting compliance from his staff based on his position alone. This approach was ineffective and alienated his team.

As George started to build relationships based on trust and mutual respect, he harnessed the power of informal authority. He listened to Sandy, acknowledged the insights of the new hires, and fostered a collaborative environment. This shift not only rebuilt the morale of the remaining staff but also created a culture where informal influence drove positive change.

FACING UNCERTAINTY AND EMBRACING COMPLEXITY

George's adaptive journey was marked by his acceptance of uncertainty and complexity. In the past, he sought straightforward solutions and resisted the unpredictable nature of trust. However, the crisis forced him to embrace a more flexible and open-minded approach.

By acknowledging that not all problems had immediate or simple solutions, George encouraged experimentation and learning from embracing risk. This mindset allowed him and his team to navigate complex challenges more directly, adapt to changing circumstances, and remain resilient in the face of adversity.

CREATING WIN-WIN SOLUTIONS

Throughout his journey, George learned the importance of creating win-win solutions. Instead of imposing top-down decisions, he started to seek input from all stakeholders, ensuring that changes were beneficial for everyone involved. For example, the initiative to second brokers to the trust company allowed for cross-functional learning and fostered a deeper understanding of the trust business among brokerage staff. This initiative not only improved trust services but also built stronger interdepartmental relationships, creating a more cohesive and collaborative environment.

REFLECTING ON THE JOURNEY

Looking back over the ten years since the crisis, George was blown away by the magnitude of the changes they had gone through. The once isolated and autocratic leader had become a champion of adaptive change, leading a thriving trust company with an adaptive culture that promoted continuous learning and improvement. The positive feedback loops from audits and exams, the growth in trust accounts, and the retention of skilled staff were testaments to the power of adaptive change they had implemented as a team.

George prided himself on saving Sandy and the trust company, but he humbly acknowledged that it was Sandy and Bob who had truly saved him. Their insights and willingness to help were crucial in his journey. Through their support, George had learned to embrace adaptive challenges, continually question his assumptions, and build a resilient and dynamic organization.

In the end, George's story is a powerful reminder that true leadership is about being willing to change oneself, seeking the right help, leveraging informal authority, embracing uncertainty, and creating solutions that benefit all. By doing all of these things, George not only vanquished the Invisible Threat but also set a new standard for adaptive leadership in the trust and wealth management industry.

VANQUISHING THE THREAT

Before we end this final chapter, let's reflect on the journey we've taken together. Throughout, we've explored the intricate challenges and adaptive strategies necessary to navigate the ever-evolving landscape of the professional fiduciary industry as it exists in today's modern wealth management landscape. From looking through the right lens and identifying hidden assumptions to leveraging informal authority and embracing adaptive change, we've laid out a roadmap to clear the fog and vanquish the Invisible Threat within your organization.

In George's story, we saw firsthand how adaptive change can not only help an individual to change, it can transform an entire organization. His journey from rigid thinking to embracing a collaborative and adaptive approach serves as a powerful example of what's possible when we can see through the right lens to challenge our hidden assumptions, seek the right help, and enter the gate to an adaptive culture.

As we look to the future, let's keep in mind that our journey doesn't end here. The insights and strategies we've discussed are not just theoretical concepts but practical tools you can apply to your unique circumstances. Whether you're a leader, a team member, or an informal authority within your organization, realize that you do have the power to provoke meaningful change.

Now that you understand more about counterintuitive ideas and how to use them to push Leverage Points in the right direction, your adaptive journey ahead promises to be delightfully challenging. We call on you to embrace an adaptive mindset and even become "the right help" yourself for others. But we also caution you to remain vigilant for those times when another fog may settle in to hide yet another Invisible Threat.

Finally, we challenge you to use your power—your informal

authority—to build on, and improve, our wonderful, fascinating, and ever-expanding professional fiduciary services industry.

You are instrumental in ensuring that our grand fiduciary business will have the resilience to meet the needs of its stakeholders—those grantors and beneficiaries relying on your perpetual success in administering the trusts of the future—and that ours will be an industry that can vanquish the Invisible Threat and thrive to serve its clients for generations to come.

LET'S BUILD SOMETHING TOGETHER

ERE WE ARE, AT THE END OF OUR JOURNEY, AMIDST A fragmented wealth management regulatory landscape. Despite our hopes, little has changed from a regulatory perspective in the post-Gramm–Leach–Bliley Act era. The same confusion that existed before the Great Recession of 2007–2009 persists today, despite the good intentions behind the Dodd–Frank Act to improve the financial stability of the US, along with other regulatory efforts. With recent legislative energy focusing on anti-terrorism and anti-money laundering measures through the Corporate Transparency Act, comprehensive and complementary regulatory frameworks for all players in the wealth management industry remains mired in fog.

We wrote this book to help professional fiduciary firms tackle the Invisible Threat. We know our trust industry is filled with good, well-intentioned professionals struggling to navigate in the broader wealth management industry. Especially for newcomers to this line of work, it can feel like operating in an eternal muddle. Yes, there have been changes and guidance provided over the past twenty years, but these have mostly just led to more confusion.

In fact, when it comes to the wealth management industry, all too often it feels like we've been left with a bunch of puzzle pieces and no box-cover picture to guide us. What is the finished puzzle supposed to look like? No one really knows.

Consider this: ask ten professionals to define "wealth management" or "fiduciary," and you'll get ten different answers. Easier still, just Google it and scroll through the plethora of different opinions and explanations you'll get. This inconsistency breeds mistrust, lawsuits, and regulatory sanctions and penalties. The patchwork of rules across the fifty states and state and federal regulatory bodies leaves a fragmented regulatory system that has not kept up with developments in the wealth management industry, making compliance a nightmare for providers and true customer protection difficult for clients.

These inconsistencies are not just theoretical. They erode trust and stability, shaking our confidence in the foundations of our country's financial institutions. Managing people's life savings demands the highest of standards.

Justice Cardozo's words used to describe the duty of loyalty imposed upon a fiduciary—"Something stricter than the morals of the market place. Not honesty alone, but the punctilio of an honor most sensitive, is then the standard of behavior."[36]—have endured for decades and continue to set the highest bar for the trust industry. Yet it's an industry that relies still on the morals and honor, the individual integrity, of those who labor in it. There's not a consistent requirement for entering the profession, never mind clear rules for precisely how those who work for, or with, professional fiduciary firms must act when there exist conflicting priorities between diverse regulated affiliates under the same corporate organization. This lack of clarity damages everyone involved—service providers and clients alike.

It doesn't have to be this way. Imagine a future where all fiduciaries are required to obtain standardized certification, ensuring high ethical and professional standards. This would not only build trust but also elevate the entire industry. There are ongoing attempts on the part of our government to do precisely that, but they remain bogged down in the post-GLBA era of combined bank-regulated and securities-regulated financial services firms working under one corporate holding company. These regulatory silos are, of course, then subject to intense political pressures. Being a legislator for today's modern wealth management industry can't be an easy task! But more to the point, where does this all leave you? How do you know where to even stand?

As an informal authority in your organization, you don't have to just wait for the hammer to fall. You hold the power to provoke the change. To set high standards for transparency and conduct. To be a flag bearer for your professional fiduciary firm and others, toward rebuilding trust and transforming the industry.

You know, and your clients know: consumers of today's financial services deserve better. The broad wealth management industry should be guided by experts who prioritize their clients' assets above their own. And you are now in a position to deliver what clients deserve. While the financial world won't change overnight, the lessons in this book provide a roadmap. As these insights become internalized, imbedded in organizational frameworks, even if just one professional fiduciary firm at a time, they will radiate outward, influencing others, eventually clearing the fog and reaching the diverse silos in the broader wealth management industry.

This isn't just one fight on the part of professional fiduciary firms. It's a grander battle that must waged on behalf of everyone: providers, legislators, regulators, and consumers.

Together, let's each do our part to clear the fog and banish the Invisible Threat for good.

We leave you now with our six-part diagnosis/prescription for industry transformation.

Here's what you need to know, in a nutshell:

1. The Invisible Threat still looms large, underscoring the urgent need for clear, unified standards in wealth management.
2. The industry lacks a consistent definition and understanding of key terms like "wealth management" and "fiduciary."
3. The inconsistent regulatory environment harms both providers and consumers, leading to mistrust and instability.
4. There is an urgent need for standardized qualifications and certifications for fiduciaries.
5. Proactive leadership within the industry can drive significant positive change.
6. Informed and proactive consumers can play a crucial role in driving improvements in the wealth management industry.

APPENDIX

GLOSSARY OF TERMS

GLOSSARY OF TERMS—*LISTED BY CHAPTER*

INTRODUCTION

1. Technical Work: A problem-solving approach involving clear, well-defined issues with straightforward solutions, often managed by experts.
2. Adaptive Work: A problem-solving approach requiring organizational or individual changes in behavior, mindset, or beliefs to address complex, ambiguous challenges.
3. silos: Organizational structures where departments or sectors operate independently from one another, often leading to inefficiencies or lack of collaboration.
4. holding environment: A concept where a leader or organization provides a sense of safety and support during times of change or uncertainty, allowing individuals to tackle adaptive challenges.
5. formal authority: The official power granted to individuals, based on their position or role within an organization, typ-

ically responsible for making decisions and implementing technical solutions.

6. informal authority: The influence an individual derives from their expertise, credibility, and trust within an organization, rather than an official title or position. Informal authority plays a critical role in navigating adaptive challenges.

7. Invisible Threat: The unseen risks and hidden assumptions within organizations that can lead to instability, particularly in fiduciary and wealth management settings.

8. hidden assumptions: Unspoken, often unconscious beliefs or practices within an organization that can undermine its operations or lead to failure.

CHAPTER 1

1. blind spots: Areas of ignorance or unawareness that prevent individuals or organizations from seeing the full picture or understanding the root cause of a problem.

2. Fiduciary Lens (big-F Fiduciary Lens): The perspective taken by professional fiduciary firms that places emphasis on the fiduciary responsibilities toward the trust and its beneficiaries, distinct from the small-f fiduciary approach of other financial services firms.

3. small-f fiduciary: The fiduciary responsibilities typically carried out by financial advisors or broker-dealers, focusing on client relationships rather than the trust entity itself.

4. Whack-a-Mole: A metaphor used to describe a situation where multiple problems continually arise, and as one is addressed, another immediately pops up, creating an ongoing struggle to maintain control.

5. ill-suited business combinations: The merging of different financial service entities, such as brokerage firms and trust

companies, that may not fit well together in terms of culture, philosophy, or business operations.

6. estate and gift tax laws: Laws governing the taxation of wealth transfers through estates or gifts, which can impact the trust business, especially during periods of legal changes.

7. client relationships (ownership of client): The assumption in financial services that the advisor or broker has control over the client relationship, often causing conflict with fiduciary duties.

CHAPTER 2

1. lens: A metaphorical term for a particular perspective or mindset through which individuals or organizations view their problems or environment.

2. right help: External support or guidance that is not only competent but also well-suited to address both the surface-level and deeper, systemic issues within an organization.

3. 3' Prime Option: A decision-making approach that focuses on changing the person or organization with the problem, as opposed to applying standard technical solutions.

4. adaptive work avoidance: The tendency of individuals or organizations to avoid engaging in necessary Adaptive Work by focusing on surface-level problems and technical solutions.

5. resilience: The ability of an organization or individual to adapt to challenges and maintain progress despite setbacks, particularly in the context of long-term solutions.

6. threshold: A critical point or stage at which an organization or individual must make a significant change to overcome challenges or advance to a new level.

CHAPTER 3

1. gatekeepers: Individuals or groups (e.g., Board members, committees, management) responsible for overseeing the execution of fiduciary duties within a professional fiduciary firm. They act as monitors and decision-makers for trust operations.
2. letting-go: The process of acknowledging the limits of one's knowledge and releasing old assumptions and beliefs to embrace adaptive change.
3. entering the gate: The moment when an individual or organization acknowledges the need for adaptive change, letting go of prior knowledge, assumptions, and behaviors to address new, complex challenges.

CHAPTER 4

1. wealth management: A broad and often vaguely defined industry that offers comprehensive financial services, including trust administration, investment management, estate planning, and tax strategies.
2. wealth management contradiction: A dilemma within professional fiduciary firms where the interests of a wealth management organization and the fiduciary duty to trust beneficiaries conflict.
3. grantor: The individual who creates a trust by transferring assets into it. In irrevocable trusts, the grantor often loses control over the assets, even though they may still feel like they are the client.
4. win-win solution: An outcome where both sides of a conflict or challenge benefit without compromise, often the goal of an adaptive solution.
5. mermaids: The good things in the current environment

that people want to keep when facing change or adaptive challenges.

6. alligators: The dangerous or problematic aspects of the current environment that need to be eliminated to achieve adaptive success.

7. pots of gold: The benefits or positive aspects of a future environment that come with embracing adaptive change.

8. crutches: The risks or potential challenges in the future environment that need to be managed when adopting adaptive solutions.

CHAPTER 5

1. formal authority: The official power granted to individuals, based on their position or role within an organization, typically responsible for making decisions and implementing technical solutions.

2. informal authority: The influence an individual derives from their expertise, credibility, and trust within an organization, rather than an official title or position. Informal authority plays a critical role in navigating adaptive challenges.

3. Goldratt Change Matrix: A framework for overcoming resistance to change by identifying positive aspects (mermaids), negative aspects (alligators), benefits of the future (pots of gold), and challenges of change (crutches), used to guide adaptive solutions.

CHAPTER 6

1. provoking change: The deliberate act of injecting stress or raising the level of discomfort within an organization to motivate others toward addressing issues, implementing

improvements, or driving adaptive change. This is done through informal authority rather than formal mandates.

2. thermostat effect: A metaphor used to describe the role of the provoker in adjusting the level of pressure or stress within an organization, similar to raising or lowering the heat, to drive problem-solving and innovation without overwhelming the team.

3. adaptive capacity: The ability of individuals or organizations to embrace and manage change effectively, often by collaborating, innovating, and overcoming adaptive challenges that require new ways of thinking and acting.

4. optimal conflict: The point at which individuals or organizations are pushed to the edge of their existing knowledge or comfort zones, creating a conflict or tension that drives creativity, growth, and breakthrough solutions.

5. Structured Discomfort: A concept referring to the intentional introduction of stress or pressure in a controlled way to push individuals or teams beyond their comfort zones and encourage adaptive change.

6. breakthrough solutions: Significant progress made toward resolving an adaptive challenge. These solutions may not be elegant or perfect but often lead to strengthening resilience, embracing discomfort, or setting ambitious goals.

CHAPTER 7

1. adaptive culture: A workplace environment that embraces continuous change and improvement by pushing beyond comfort zones and setting audacious goals, encouraging collaboration, innovation, and risk-taking.

2. inertia: The internal resistance within an organization to change or move beyond the status quo, often caused by

applying technical solutions to adaptive challenges or an over-reliance on stability.

3. Audacious Goal-Setting: A strategic approach where individuals or organizations set bold, seemingly impossible objectives that compel collaboration and innovative thinking, far beyond what they can achieve alone.

4. POOGI (Process of Ongoing Improvement): A methodology introduced by Dr. Eli Goldratt, promoting continuous improvement and adaptive change by encouraging individuals and organizations to strive to do better, even in small increments.

5. Enduring Adaptive Solution: A long-term, sustainable solution that not only addresses current challenges but also strengthens an organization's capacity to continue adapting to future changes and challenges.

CHAPTER 8

1. changing the system: A process of altering an organization's underlying processes, values, and internal mechanisms to ensure lasting adaptive change rather than just addressing surface-level problems.

2. good problem: A dilemma that reveals the limits of current understanding and drives transformation by pushing individuals or organizations into optimal conflict, ultimately resulting in greater benefits and growth than initially expected.

3. grasp greater than your reach: The idea that the outcomes or insights gained from tackling a problem exceed the original goal or scope of the solution, leading to deeper understanding and broader application.

4. feedback loops: Mechanisms for continuously assessing performance and outcomes, such as fiduciary risk assess-

ments and audits, which provide valuable information that helps organizations maintain adaptive success and ensure an enduring solution.

CHAPTER 9

1. vanquishing the Invisible Threat: The process of identifying and eliminating the unseen barriers, assumptions, and misalignments within an organization that hinder its ability to achieve success.
2. Leverage Points: Specific areas within an organization where applying targeted effort or change can produce significant results, leading to system-wide improvements.
3. Counterintuitive Solutions: Ideas or actions that go against conventional wisdom but are essential for overcoming complex challenges, particularly in adaptive change contexts.

GLOSSARY OF TERMS—*LISTED ALPHABETICALLY*

3′ Prime Option: A decision-making approach that focuses on changing the person or organization with the problem, as opposed to applying standard technical solutions

adaptive capacity: The ability of individuals or organizations to embrace and manage change effectively, often by collaborating, innovating, and overcoming adaptive challenges that require new ways of thinking and acting.

adaptive culture: A workplace environment that embraces continuous change and improvement by pushing beyond comfort zones and setting audacious goals, encouraging collaboration, innovation, and risk-taking.

adaptive work: A problem-solving approach requiring organizational or individual changes in behavior, mindset, or beliefs to address complex, ambiguous challenges.

adaptive work avoidance: The tendency of individuals or organizations to avoid engaging in necessary Adaptive work by focusing on surface-level problems and technical solutions.

alligators: The dangerous or problematic aspects of the current environment that need to be eliminated to achieve adaptive success.

Audacious Goal-Setting: A strategic approach where individuals or organizations set bold, seemingly impossible objectives that compel collaboration and innovative thinking, far beyond what they can achieve alone.

blind spots: Areas of ignorance or unawareness that prevent individuals or organizations from seeing the full picture or understanding the root cause of a problem.

breakthrough solutions: Significant progress made toward resolving an adaptive challenge. These solutions may not be elegant or perfect but often lead to strengthening resilience, embracing discomfort, or setting ambitious goals.

changing the system: A process of altering an organization's underlying processes, values, and internal mechanisms to ensure lasting adaptive change rather than just addressing surface-level problems.

client relationships (Ownership of Client): The assumption in financial services that the advisor or broker has control over the client relationship, often causing conflict with fiduciary duties.

Counterintuitive Solutions: Ideas or actions that go against conventional wisdom but are essential for overcoming complex challenges, particularly in adaptive change context.

crutches: The risks or potential challenges in the future environment that need to be managed when adopting adaptive solutions.

Enduring Adaptive Solution: A long-term, sustainable solution that not only addresses current challenges but also strengthens an organization's capacity to continue adapting to future changes and challenges.

entering the gate: The moment when an individual or organization acknowledges the need for adaptive change, letting go of prior knowledge, assumptions, and behaviors to address new, complex challenges.

estate and gift tax laws: Laws governing the taxation of wealth transfers through estates or gifts, which can impact the trust business, especially during periods of legal changes.

feedback loops: Mechanisms for continuously assessing performance and outcomes, such as fiduciary risk assessments and audits, which provide valuable information that helps organizations maintain adaptive success and ensure an enduring solution.

Fiduciary Lens (big-F Fiduciary Lens): The perspective taken by professional fiduciary firms that places emphasis on the fiduciary responsibilities toward the trust and its beneficiaries, distinct from the small-f fiduciary approach of other financial services firms.

formal authority: The official power granted to individuals, based on their position or role within an organization, typically responsible for making decisions and implementing technical solutions.

gatekeepers: Individuals or groups (e.g., Board members, committees, management) responsible for overseeing the execution of fiduciary duties within a professional fiduciary firm. They act as monitors and decision-makers for trust operations.

Goldratt Change Matrix: A framework for overcoming resistance to change by identifying positive aspects (mermaids), negative aspects (alligators), benefits of the future (pots of gold), and challenges of change (crutches), used to guide adaptive solutions.

good problem: A dilemma that reveals the limits of current understanding and drives transformation by pushing individuals or organizations into optimal conflict, ultimately resulting in greater benefits and growth than initially expected.

grasp greater than your reach: The idea that the outcomes or insights gained from tackling a problem exceed the original goal or scope of the solution, leading to deeper understanding and broader application.

grantor: The individual who creates a trust by transferring assets into it. In irrevocable trusts, the grantor often loses control over the assets, even though they may still feel like they are the client.

hidden assumptions: Unspoken, often unconscious beliefs or practices within an organization that can undermine its operations or lead to failure.

holding environment: A concept where a leader or organization provides a sense of safety and support during times of change or uncertainty, allowing individuals to tackle adaptive challenges.

ill-suited business combinations: The merging of different financial service entities, such as brokerage firms and trust companies, that may not fit well together in terms of culture, philosophy, or business operations.

inertia: The internal resistance within an organization to change or move beyond the status quo, often caused by applying technical solutions to adaptive challenges or an over-reliance on stability.

informal authority: The influence an individual derives from their expertise, credibility, and trust within an organization, rather than an official title or position. Informal authority plays a critical role in navigating adaptive challenges.

Invisible Threat: The unseen risks and hidden assumptions within organizations that can lead to instability, particularly in fiduciary and wealth management settings.

Leverage Points: Specific areas within an organization where applying targeted effort or change can produce significant results, leading to system-wide improvements.

lens: A metaphorical term for a particular perspective or mindset through which individuals or organizations view their problems or environment.

letting-go: The process of acknowledging the limits of one's knowledge and releasing old assumptions and beliefs to embrace adaptive change.

mermaids: The good things in the current environment that people want to keep when facing change or adaptive challenges.

optimal conflict: The point at which individuals or organizations are pushed to the edge of their existing knowledge or comfort zones, creating a conflict or tension that drives creativity, growth, and breakthrough solutions.

POOGI (Process of Ongoing Improvement): A methodology introduced by Dr. Eli Goldratt, promoting continuous improvement and adaptive change by encouraging individuals and organizations to strive to do better, even in small increments.

pots of gold: The benefits or positive aspects of a future environment that come with embracing adaptive change.

provoking change: The deliberate act of injecting stress or raising the level of discomfort within an organization to motivate others toward addressing issues, implementing improvements, or driving adaptive change. This is done through informal authority rather than formal mandates.

resilience: The ability of an organization or individual to adapt to challenges and maintain progress despite setbacks, particularly in the context of long-term solutions.

right help: External support or guidance that is not only competent but also well-suited to address both the surface-level and deeper, systemic issues within an organization.

silos: Organizational structures where departments or sectors operate independently from one another, often leading to inefficiencies or lack of collaboration.

small-f fiduciary: The fiduciary responsibilities typically carried out by financial advisors or broker-dealers, focusing on client relationships rather than the trust entity itself.

Structured Discomfort: A concept referring to the intentional introduction of stress or pressure in a controlled way to push individuals or teams beyond their comfort zones and encourage adaptive change.

Technical Work: A problem-solving approach involving clear, well-defined issues with straightforward solutions, often managed by experts.

thermostat effect: A metaphor used to describe the role of the provoker in adjusting the level of pressure or stress within an organization, similar to raising or lowering the heat, to drive problem-solving and innovation without overwhelming the team.

threshold: A critical point or stage at which an organization or individual must make a significant change to overcome challenges or advance to a new level.

vanquishing the Invisible Threat: The process of identifying and eliminating the unseen barriers, assumptions, and misalignments within an organization that hinder its ability to achieve success.

wealth management: A broad and often vaguely defined industry that offers comprehensive financial services, including trust administration, investment management, estate planning, and tax strategies.

wealth management contradiction: A dilemma within professional fiduciary firms where the interests of a wealth management organization and the fiduciary duty to trust beneficiaries conflict.

Whack-a-Mole: A metaphor used to describe a situation where multiple problems continually arise, and as one is addressed, another immediately pops up, creating an ongoing struggle to maintain control.

win-win solution: An outcome where both sides of a conflict or challenge benefit without compromise, often the goal of an adaptive solution.

ACKNOWLEDGMENTS

A S WE BRING THIS BOOK TO COMPLETION, WE ARE FILLED with an overwhelming sense of gratitude for the countless individuals and organizations that have enriched our lives through this journey. The greatest gift of consulting has been the opportunity to learn from those we've been privileged to work with—our clients and students—who have shared with us their experiences, insights, and wisdom over the years.

We are especially grateful to the many clients from all corners of the country, representing diverse institutions, whose challenges, ambitions, and dedication to this grand fiduciary business have inspired us to deepen our own understanding and push the boundaries of what we thought possible. Your commitment to growth, adaptive change, and trust has shaped our perspectives and has been a cornerstone in the creation of this book.

To our students and those we've mentored, you have been and continue to be constant reminders that learning is a two-way street. Your thoughtful questions, openness to new ideas, and relentless curiosity have made us better teachers and thinkers. We are privileged to have had the chance to learn alongside you and see the world through your eyes.

This book would not be what it is without the indefatigable support and patience of our incredible team at Scribe. First and foremost, Mark Chait—our guide and scribe—thank you for helping us stay true to our vision while expertly leading us through the writing process. Your keen eye kept us focused, and your ability to listen encouraged us to express ourselves in ways we hadn't anticipated. You're simply the best!

A special thanks goes out to Ellie Cole, who skillfully shepherded us through the tumultuous first months, and to Rachael Williams, who capably took the reins and brought this book to the finish line. We're also grateful to Anna Dorfman for designing our wonderful cover, and to Amy Hendrickson for her patience and guidance with the back cover copy. You are all truly terrific!

A heartfelt thank you goes out to our Blurbers! Hale Mast, Haris Khan, Carter Wilcoxson, and Gavin Finlay, who each graciously agreed to have their spirited words featured on the cover of our book. We are grateful to these special friends and industry leaders. Your thoughtful words are truly inspirational, and we can't thank you enough for this honor.

We also offer a humble thank you to our friends and family, particularly those mentioned in this book. We apologize if our memories of the past don't match yours—we all interpret and treasure moments from our past in our own ways. And with each passing year those memories will have faded and melded with others in mysterious ways. At the end of it all, though, we enjoyed the opportunity this book brought us to relive those memories and we know you will forgive us any lapses in our recall.

And of course, as authors typically do, we'd each like to thank our respective spouses for their patience and support through the book writing process. But as co-authors, we journeyed through this process together—we cried, we fought, we laughed, we nearly gave up, we gave each other hope. When one of us stumbled, the other was right there to keep us going. We know that without both spouses supporting each other in our efforts to co-author this book, it truly would never have happened. So, thank you and thank you.

Finally, we'd like to thank Ben. You know what you mean to each of us. We are honored and excited you have also chosen this grand fiduciary business for your career and have dedicated this book to you. We are proud as we watch you continue to learn and grow and humbled that you reach out to us for guidance from time to time. Thank you for being you.

ABOUT THE AUTHORS

MATT AND JOANNE EBY are the founders of Nth Degree Financial Solutions, a premier consulting firm established in 2000. For over two decades, they have worked closely with fiduciary firms, bringing deep expertise to areas such as facilitating strategic change, navigating complex regulatory landscapes, and securing trust company licenses.

As accomplished speakers and presenters, Matt and Joanne excel in creating custom solutions and training programs tailored to their clients' needs. They understand that the real challenges of this industry often lie beneath the surface, in the nuances and uncertainties that standard business practices don't always address. Through their work, they aim to help their clients do more than simply survive—they empower them to successfully exceed expectations, fostering a mindset of continuous growth and adaptation.

The Ebys believe that long-term success in fiduciary services isn't achieved by following the status quo but by embracing complexity with integrity and resilience. Their mission is about more than just compliance; it's about fostering a culture of integrity, resilience, and trust, where providers and practitioners are empowered to do what's right, especially when it's not easy.

NOTES

1   Joseph Karl Grant, "What the Financial Services Industry Puts Together Let No Person Put Asunder: How the Gramm–Leach–Bliley Act Contributed to the 2008–2009 American Capital Markets Crisis," *Albany Law Review* (2010): 371–420, https://ssrn.com/abstract=1525670. In his article, Grant cites Senator Patrick Leahy (D-VT) as saying, "Modernizing current law will make the financial services industry more competitive, both at home and abroad. This legislation will make it easier for banking, securities, and insurance firms to consolidate their services, allowing them to cut expenses and offer more products at a lower cost to businesses and consumers." Grant also cites Senator Bryan (R-NV) as echoing the notion of one-stop shopping when he noted: "We will provide new convenience to the American public, we will have one-stop shopping for insurance, banking and securities; that it will be less expensive; that more options will be provided" (385–386, note 56).

2   Melissa Lin, "Glass–Steagall Act: Did Its Repeal Cause the Financial Crisis?," Toptal, accessed September 14, 2024.

3   Note, per Lin's article, "The repeal ushered in a period of mega-mergers. The new six largest banks grew their assets from 20% of GDP in 1997 to over 60% of GDP in 2008." Lin, "Glass–Steagall Act."

4   Quoted in Lin, "Glass–Steagall Act."

5   Under the Bank Holding Company Act, a bank holding company may elect to be a financial holding company (FHC). The Federal Reserve's National Information Center (NIC) website can be used to search for bank holding companies that have elected to be treated as FHCs. See "Financial Holding Companies," Board of Governors of the Federal Reserve System, updated March 6, 2017, https://www.federalreserve.gov/supervisionreg/fhc.htm.

6   Ronald Heifetz, *Leadership Without Easy Answers*, (Belknap Press, 1996), 87.

7   "FINRA Regulates Broker-Dealers, Capital Acquisition Brokers and Funding Portals. A Broker-Dealer is in the business of buying or selling securities on behalf of its customers or its own account or both. A Capital Acquisition Broker is a Broker-Dealer subject to a narrower rule book. A Funding Portal is a crowdfunding intermediary." See "Firms We Regulate," FINRA, accessed June 19, 2024, https://www.finra.org/about/firms-we-regulate.

8 "The SEC regulates investment advisers who manage $110 million or more in client assets, while state securities regulators have jurisdiction over advisers who manage up to $100 million. Advisers with less than $100 million in assets under management (AUM) must register with the state regulator for the state where the adviser has its principal place of business." See "Investment Advisors," FINRA, accessed June 19, 2024, https://www.finra.org/investors/investing/working-with-investment-professional/investment-advisers.

9 Lin, "Glass–Steagall Act." Lin writes, "Still, there is credence in an oft-overlooked, indirect cause of the Act's absence: the creation of a reckless, risk-taking, profit-focused culture on Wall Street. In fact, economic Nobel Prize laureate Joseph Stiglitz included this cultural shift as one of his five major contributing factors to the recession: The most important consequence of the repeal of Glass–Steagall was indirect—it lay in the way repeal changed an entire culture [...] When the repeal of Glass–Steagall brought investment and commercial banks together, the investment-bank culture came out on top. There was a demand for the kind of high returns that could be obtained only through high leverage and big risk taking.'"

10 Lin, "Glass–Steagall Act." Lin writes, "This mindset and resulting reckless culture, though intangible, were undoubtedly real. As some experts assert, the investment banking culture of risk-taking, focus on short-term profits, and deprioritization of client interests was at the heart of the crisis—which may not have been present, or would at least have been minimized, with Glass–Steagall."

11 After the repeal of the Glass–Steagall Act, a bank holding company could engage directly in, or establish or acquire subsidiaries that engaged in, non-banking activities closely related to banking, such as mortgage banking, consumer and commercial finance and loan servicing, leasing, collection agency, asset management, trust company, real estate appraisal, financial and investment advisory activities, management consulting, employee benefits consulting, career counseling services, and certain insurance-related activities. The GLBA also amended the Bank Holding Company Act to allow a bank holding company to declare itself a financial holding company, which is a hybrid form of a bank holding company, and thereby engage in financial activities—activities not closely related to banking—including securities underwriting and dealing, insurance agency and underwriting activities, and merchant banking activities. Post-GLBA, the number of bank and financial holding companies has expanded to the point where most U.S. banks are part of a bank holding company, with 100 percent of large banks with more than $10 billion in assets owned through such legal holding company structures.

12 Ayoob Rawat Kabir and Rawat, "Wealth," Private Wealth & Family Office Association blog, August 18, 2021, https://www.pwfo.org/blog/wealth.

13 We are grateful to our colleague, who prefers to remain unnamed, for their permission to include these words in our book.

14 Rob Cox, "A History Lesson with Merrill Deal," *The New York Times*, January 22, 2009.

15 "Overcoming Resistance to Change—Isn't It Obvious," July 17, 2010, by Learning TOC (Theory of Constraints), YouTube, 6 min., 13 sec., https://www.youtube.com/watch?v=hcz1aZ6ok7w. See also Eliyahu M. Goldratt, *Isn't It Obvious: Retailing and the Theory of Constraints* (pub. by author, 2010).

16 Formerly known as the John Marshall Law School.

17 Piet Hein, "Small Things & Great," Grooks, accessed May 15, 2024, https://www.archimedes-lab.org/grooks.html.

18 Kelley R. Taylor, "SECURE 2.0 Act Summary: New Retirement Plan Rules to Know," Kiplinger, updated June 25, 2024, https://www.kiplinger.com/retirement/bipartisan-retirement-savings-package-in-massive-budget-bill.

19   *FAQs about Retirement Plans and ERISA*, US Department of Labor Employee Benefits Security
       Administration, accessed May 27, 2024, https://www.dol.gov/sites/dolgov/files/ebsa/about-ebsa/
       our-activities/resource-center/faqs/retirement-plans-and-erisa-compliance.pdf.

20   *Publication 590-B (2023), Distributions from Individual Retirement Arrangements (IRAs)*,
       Department of the Treasury, Internal Revenue Service, https://www.irs.gov/pub/irs-prior/
       p590b--2023.pdf.

21   "Secure Retirement Legislation Becomes Law: Overview of Provisions Affecting Retirement
       Plans," Morgan Lewis, December 23, 2019, https://www.morganlewis.com/pubs/2019/12/
       secure-retirement-legislation-becomes-law-overview-of-provisions-affecting-retirement-plans.

22   Ed Slott, "Be Aware of These New Rules for Inherited IRAs: Tax and IRA Expert Ed
       Slott Discusses Whether There's Any Way to Lessen the Tax Bill," interview by Christine
       Benz, *Morningstar*, March 20, 2024, https://www.morningstar.com/retirement/
       faqs-about-inherited-iras.

23   Slott, "Be Aware of These New Rules for Inherited IRAs."

24   Taylor, "SECURE 2.0 Act Summary." In April 2024 the IRS again delayed implementation of
       IRA RMD final rules, until 2025. Taylor writes, "With previous IRS relief, penalties are waived
       for missed RMDs from specific IRAs inherited in 2020, 2021, 2022, and 2023."

25   "Since FinCEN was founded in 1990, it has been a key player in broad-based efforts against
       money laundering and related financial crimes. In 1995, FinCEN merged with Treasury's Office
       of Financial Enforcement and gained the responsibility for administration of the Bank Secrecy
       Act. FinCEN's mission is to provide law enforcement case support to assist in the investigation
       of money laundering and related financial crimes; to develop and administer regulations aimed
       at preventing and detecting money laundering and to pursue civil enforcement against violators
       of these rules; and to strengthen overall domestic and international efforts against money
       laundering." US Department of the Treasury, "Treasury Assistant Secretary (Enforcement)
       James E. Johnson House Banking and Financial Services Subcommittee on General Oversight
       and Investigations," press release, April 1, 1998, https://home.treasury.gov/news/press-releases/
       rr2335. For additional information, refer to www.fincen.gov.

26   *Publication 590-B (2023)*, 13.

27   On April 26, 2023 FinCEN issued a Consent Order and imposed a civil monetary penalty of $1.5
       million against Kingdom Trust Company for willful violations of the Bank Secrecy Act and its
       implementing regulations, specifically as it relates to the detection of suspicious activity and
       the filing of corresponding Suspicious Activity Reports, having determined that Kingdom Trust
       had virtually no process to identify and report suspicious transactions. This action was the
       first of its kind against a trust company. See Financial Crimes Enforcement Network, "FinCEN
       Assesses $1.5 Million Civil Money Penalty Against Kingdom Trust Company for Violations of the
       Bank Secrecy Act," press release, April 25, 2023, https://www.fincen.gov/news/news-releases/
       fincen-assesses-15-million-civil-money-penalty-against-kingdom-trust-company.

28   "Ah, but a man's reach should exceed his grasp, Or what's a heaven for?" Robert Browning,
       "Andrea del Sarto."

29   Robert Kegan and Lisa Laskow Lahey, *Immunity to Change: How to Overcome It and Unlock the
       Potential in Yourself and Your Organization* (Harvard Business Press, 2009), 167.

30   Donella H. Meadows, "Leverage Points: Places to Intervene in a System," *The Sustainability
       Institute* (1999): 1–19, https://web.archive.org/web/20131008160618/http://www.
       sustainabilityinstitute.org/pubs/Leverage_Points.pdf.

31   Meadows, "Leverage Points," 1.

32   Meadows, "Leverage Points," 1

33 Meadows, "Leverage Points."

34 Meadows, "Leverage Points."

35 Meadows, "Leverage Points," 2.

36 Meinhard v. Salmon, 249 N.Y. 458, 164 N.E. 545 (1928).